101 Answers for New Teachers and Their Mentors

Effective Teaching Tips for Daily Classroom Use

Third Edition

Annette Breaux

Routledge
Taylor & Francis Group

NEW YORK AND LONDON

Third edition published 2015
by Routledge
711 Third Avenue, New York, NY 10017

and by Routledge
2 Park Square, Milton Park, Abingdon, Oxon, OX14 4RN

Routledge is an imprint of the Taylor & Francis Group, an informa business

First edition published by Eye On Education 2003

Second edition published by Routledge 2011

Library of Congress Cataloging-in-Publication Data
Breaux, Annette L.
    101 answers for new teachers and their mentors : effective teaching tips for daily classroom use / by Annette Breaux.
        pages cm
    Includes bibliographical references.
    1. First year teachers—In-service training—Handbooks, manuals, etc.   2. Mentoring in education—Handbooks, manuals, etc.   3. Effective teaching—Handbooks, manuals, etc.   I. Title.   II. Title: One hundred one "answers" for new teachers and their mentors.   III. Title: One hundred and one "answers" for new teachers and their mentors.
    LB2844.1.N4B74   2015
    370.71′1—dc23
    2014046050

ISBN: 978-1-138-85614-1 (pbk)
ISBN: 978-1-315-71986-3 (ebk)

Typeset in Palatino
by Apex CoVantage, LLC

Printed and bound in the United States of America by Sheridan Books, Inc. (a Sheridan Group Company).

Dedication

I dedicate this book to the memory of my grandfather, Pop,
the greatest teacher I have ever known.

Contents

eResources

The *Ask Yourself* questions, *Chapter Highlights*, and *Bonus Seven* from the book are also available as eResources on our website, so that you can easily download and print them for use in discussion groups, meetings, or as reminders for yourself.

You can access these resources by visiting the book product page on our website, at **www.routledge.com/books/details/9781138856141**. Then click on the tab that says "eResources," and select the files. They will begin downloading to your computer.

About the Author

Annette Breaux is one of the most entertaining and informative authors and speakers in education today. She leaves her audiences with practical techniques to implement in their classrooms immediately. Administrators agree they see results from teachers the next day.

A former classroom teacher, curriculum coordinator, and teacher induction coordinator, she was also the author of Louisiana FIRST, a statewide induction program for new teachers. Annette has also co-authored books with two of education's greats – Harry Wong and Todd Whitaker.

Her other writings published by Routledge include *REAL Teachers, REAL Challenges, REAL Solutions*; *Seven Simple Secrets: What the BEST Teachers Know and Do!*; *50 Ways to Improve Student Behavior: Simple Solutions to Complex Challenges*; *Making Good Teaching Great: Everyday Strategies for Teaching with Impact*, and *101 Poems for Teachers*. She also has two books published by Jossey-Bass: *The Ten-Minute Inservice: 40 Quick Training Sessions That Build Teacher Effectiveness* and *Quick Answers for Busy Teachers: Solutions to 60 Common Challenges*.

Teachers who have read Annette's writings or heard her speak agree that they come away with user-friendly information, heartfelt inspiration, and a much-needed reminder that theirs is the noblest of all professions.

Foreword

This book is THE book I wish I had had when I first started teaching. Like most new teachers, I had more questions than answers. Any experienced teacher will readily tell you, "If only I had known then what I know now. . . ." Consider the following:

- **New teachers need support**, from day one, if they are going to succeed in their classrooms. Teaching is new to them, so most of their experiences will be first-time experiences!

- Although many new teachers do receive structured, ongoing **induction support** provided by their schools or districts, still many do not. Regardless, new teachers require and appreciate as much support as we can provide.

- **Many mentors receive one-shot training and nothing more**. The more training a mentor receives, the better he or she is able to mentor. However, a mentor is only ONE person, usually with his or her own classroom. A mentor alone cannot be responsible for the success of a new teacher.

- We often tend to **assume too much regarding what new teachers are ready to handle in the classroom.**

- **New teachers want answers**, yet they are often afraid to ask for help for fear of appearing incompetent.

- In teaching, **it is as important to know what NOT to do as it is to know what TO do.** By affording new teachers ample opportunities to learn from the rich experiences of others, we help them avoid costly mistakes.

- There are **simple and basic teaching strategies that can help any teacher to be more effective.** New teachers deserve access to all of these from day one!

This book provides answers to typical new-teacher questions, simple solutions to common classroom challenges, and tips that will help new teachers be better teachers, and mentors be better teachers and mentors. If you are neither a new teacher nor a mentor, read on anyway, because the strategies in this book can benefit any teacher seeking to be more effective. I share this book with you along with my love of children, my love of teaching, my knowledge that teachers touch lives, and my absolute conviction that every child is someone special. Every student deserves a capable, competent, caring teacher.

New to the Third Edition

- ◆ Advice on incorporating technology effectively into your lessons.
- ◆ Tips for using social media appropriately to connect with others.
- ◆ *Ask Yourself* questions (included in each tip) and *Chapter Highlights* (following each chapter) to help you apply the ideas in your own classroom. These resources are available both in the book and on our website so that you can download them and use them in discussion groups, in mentor/new-teacher meetings, or as reminders to post wherever you'd like.
- ◆ A *bonus section* with simple, succinct, informative lists of what the most effective teachers do (on a daily basis) to deal with students, parents, and co-workers effectively.

Introduction

To the Teacher

Do you love children? Do you want to make a difference? Do you want to have a positive impact on young lives? Of course you do! That's why you've chosen to teach. But know that teaching asks a lot of you. It requires patience, commitment, dedication, love of children, charisma, confidence, and competence. **And it affords you the platform to affect the lives of all of your students on a daily basis.**

If you are a new teacher, you know that it is your sincere desire to be successful, to inspire, to touch lives, and to make a difference. Yet many of you, through no fault of your own, lack the necessary training to be effective from your very first day of teaching. Hopefully, you have signed on with a school district that provides induction training. Induction is a highly structured, systematic means of training and supporting new teachers, beginning before their first day of teaching and continuing throughout their first two or three years. Mentoring is one vital component of the induction process. **If you have not been assigned a mentor, find one.** There are many capable, competent, caring teachers out there who are more than willing to share their expertise with novices. **You cannot and will not be expected to know everything from day one.** You'll need guidance. And although mentors cannot provide for all of the needs of new teachers, they can be valuable assets to new teachers. So seek out the most positive, enthusiastic, successful teacher on the faculty and enlist his or her support to help ensure your success in the classroom.

Remember: you are helping to mold the future, and your influence will long outlive you. You are a teacher. What an honor, and what a tremendous responsibility. Rise to the challenge!

To the Mentor

If you have been selected to serve as a mentor for a new teacher, you should be honored. Someone, somewhere, has recognized your successes in the classroom and your leadership qualities. And, hopefully, you have been well trained in the art of mentoring. If not, please insist on it! **No matter how good your teaching skills may be, mentoring is different from teaching, and it requires structured training.**

As a mentor, you will play the role of teacher, friend, guide, coach, and role model. You will be expected to provide support, encouragement, a listening ear, a welcoming shoulder, constructive feedback, and suggestions for improvement. You will be required to exhibit professionalism, the ability to plan and organize, a love of children and teaching, excellence in teaching, effective communication skills, coaching skills, conferencing skills, and an optimistic attitude. You will be responsible for maintaining confidentiality; sharing knowledge, skills, and information with the new teacher; meeting frequently with the new teacher; observing the new teacher; providing demonstration lessons for the new teacher; familiarizing the new teacher with school policies, procedures, and culture; and participating in ongoing professional improvement activities. And above all, you must be understanding, supportive, trustworthy, empathetic, innovative, knowledge-able, open-minded, reform-minded, and committed.

Does this sound overwhelming? Well rest assured that your efforts will be rewarded a hundred-fold, as **you will be positively affecting the lives of the new teachers you mentor. This will have a direct impact on every student who will ever enter the new teachers' classroom doors.**

Congratulations on being selected to mentor a new teacher, and thank you for accepting the challenge.

Common New-teacher Challenges

Although all new teachers face a variety of challenges in the classroom, there are several that seem common to most. In fact, these are the same challenges that remain common for many veteran teachers throughout their careers. These challenges include dealing with the overall management of the classroom; effectively handling discipline problems; dealing with challenging students, co-workers, and parents; planning effectively; managing time wisely; remaining calm and professional in the face of unnerving situations; using the most effective teaching strategies; accommodating individual differences in students; engaging students in critical thinking, and using technology appropriately and effectively.

This book is specifically designed to assist teachers in dealing with the aforementioned challenges simply and effectively. It is not loaded with fads, trends, educational jargon of the day, or the latest of educational innovations. Rather, it provides tried-and-true techniques that will work for anyone willing to implement them. Quite simply, this book will help enhance teaching and learning at any grade level. The opportunity to be the most effective teacher you can be awaits you, and the fact that you are reading this book says that you are seizing that opportunity and welcoming the challenge.

How to Use This Book

This book may be used in one of several ways. It is designed primarily **to provide ideas and promote effective teaching for both new teachers and mentors,** and to facilitate discussion between mentors and new teachers. Of course, the ideas and teaching tips are universal and may be used by any teacher seeking to be more effective. The 101 tips are divided into the following sections: *Classroom Management, Planning, Instruction, Professionalism, Motivation and Rapport,* and *A Teacher's Influence.* If a new teacher is working on establishing effective classroom management, he or she should use the suggestions found under that section. If a mentor needs to "brush up" on management skills so as to serve as a role model for the new teacher, the tips found there will prove beneficial. Feel free to pick and choose any and all that seem appropriate for your classroom. However, use all of them if you want to truly enhance your teaching whether you are a mentor, a first-time teacher, or any teacher seeking to better your skills.

Again, **the very fact that you are reading this says that you are a dedicated teacher who chooses to make a difference in the lives of the students you teach.** This book will help you do just that.

Section One

Classroom Management

How Does One Manage a Classroom?

"How does one manage a classroom? Is it really rocket science?
For I've been told it's difficult to control so much student defiance."
Well, management is about the teacher, and what the teacher expects
Because everything about the teacher absolutely affects
How students will or won't respond, how they will or will not act,
And with excellent classroom management, students behave well.
  That's a fact!
So set clear rules and procedures, and show how you want things done
And remember that on the scale of importance, being consistent is
  number one!
Consistent in how you treat each one, consistent in your preparation,
Consistent in being professional, regardless of your level of frustration,
Consistent in saying what you mean and in meaning what you say,
Consistent in making every student feel special every day,
Consistent in your refusal to give up on anyone,
Consistent in helping students to see a task through 'til it's done,
Consistent with a good attitude, for your attitude sets the tone,
Consistent in being available, so that no student feels alone,
Consistent in helping every child to know he can succeed,
Being consistent is the key to classroom management, indeed!
It really is not difficult – just be consistent at being consistent –
And soon your discipline problems will be a memory that is distant!

Tip 1
Start the Year Successfully

Since you never get a second chance to make a first impression,
please take care that what you wear is a positive expression!

First impressions are vital! **In the classroom, your first impression can set the tone for the entire school year.** Often, teachers make the mistake of diving into "teaching the content" from the very first day of school. Instead, it is critically important that you take the time to let the students know who you are, that you allow them the opportunity to begin to tell you who they are, and that you immediately set them up for success. One way to do this is through structure. If you are going through new-teacher induction training, then you already know how your first day of school should be structured. If not, find out from your mentor teacher or other successful veteran teachers exactly what they do on the first day of school. You can also connect, online, with other educators who post their lists, tips, reminders, and procedures for a successful first-day experience.

Here are a few MUSTS for **beginning the school year on a positive note**:

- Greet your students at the door with a huge smile on your face.
- Be organized and prepared. Plan every minute of your first day beforehand.
- Have some type of appealing assignment (possibly an interest inventory) awaiting students so that they can get busy immediately upon entering the classroom.
- Remain calm, pleasant, and positive. If you're smiling, they won't know you're nervous!
- Share your expectations and tell them what they can expect from you and your class.
- Tell them you are so excited to be their teacher, and thank them for being in your class.
- Express your belief that they will ALL be successful!

✔ **Ask Yourself:** Do I have a plan in place for my first day that will immediately give my students the message that I care, that this class is organized and structured, and that they will succeed and have fun this year?

Tip 2
Make Classroom Management a Priority

*Without procedures and routines, certain chaos
intervenes. But when students know exactly what's
expected, behavior problems are often corrected.*

Contrary to popular belief, **discipline is NOT the number one problem in the classroom.** Rather, **the lack of clear, structured, well-rehearsed procedures and routines is what causes most discipline problems.** Thus, from day one, effective teachers establish clear routines and procedures, and students are shown and told exactly what is expected of them. These teachers are also aware of the fact that the term **"classroom management" refers to everything you do to make your classroom run smoothly**: how you arrange the furniture to facilitate learning, how you expect students to enter and exit the classroom, where you stand when you are teaching to ensure that you are in close proximity to all of your students, how you pace your activities, how you establish expectations for student behavior, and so on. In other words, an effective teacher plans EVERYTHING.

If you want what all teachers want – to experience few discipline problems with your students – then it is important that you have a clear, concise classroom management plan. But please do not reinvent the wheel. Implement the basic tried-and-true management techniques of the most successful teachers – those you will continue to read about throughout this book. Aside from reading this book, you may want to read the well-known, practical, common-sense approach to classroom management: *The First Days of School* by Harry and Rosemary Wong. Also, a quick online search will yield free tips, checklists, and samples of effective management plans from fellow educators.

FACT: Just as a bus cannot transport students to school without tires, even if the bus is in perfect mechanical condition, a teacher cannot teach ANYTHING to students until classroom management is in place, even if he or she is knowledgeable about the content. Management is just as important to learning as tires are to getting a bus from point A to point B. **Clearly-established procedures and routines are the most important part of any effective classroom management plan.**

✔ **Ask Yourself:** Am I clear on what I expect of my students, and do *they* know what is expected of them?

Tip 3
Have Procedures for Almost Everything

For what kinds of things should procedures be set?
For anything you don't want to regret!

Some activities lend themselves to creative expression. Others do not. *Designing* an automobile lends itself to creative expression. *Assembling* the automobile does not. On the design table, there are infinite options for how a particular automobile might be constructed. Once the final design hits the assembly line, there is now only ONE option: to follow the design plan exactly as stated. The same is true for classroom management. **In order to successfully manage a classroom of students or any group of people, clearly defined procedures – consistent ways of doing things – must be established.** Take 30 students and do not tell them how you want a task done. They will each create numerous ways to perform that task. Many of these ways will be unacceptable. You see, 30 students doing things their own way for even one task will allow for endless possibilities of how the task will be accomplished. This is good when teaching them how to think, but not so good when teaching them how to behave. So what kinds of activities require procedures in the classroom? **Any activity that does not lend itself to creative expression requires procedures.** For instance, you would not want your students "creating" ways of entering your classroom, sharpening their pencils, turning in assignments, using personal electronic devices, moving into groups, or walking to the lunchroom. As the person in charge of managing a group of students, it is your responsibility to establish procedures in order to ensure the smooth operation of your classroom environment.

The following are a few examples of activities that require procedures:

◆ Entering the classroom.
◆ Exiting the classroom.
◆ Passing in papers.
◆ Asking for permission to speak.
◆ Knowing what to do with your book bag when you enter the classroom.
◆ Asking a question.

- Working cooperatively in groups.
- Working at computer stations.
- Knowing what to do in a school lock-down, fire, or severe weather situation.
- Knowing what to do if you have finished your work and others have not.
- Turning in homework assignments.
- Using personal electronic devices in acceptable ways at acceptable times, etc.

Tell your students what you expect, show them how you expect things to be done, practice the procedures with them, and reinforce as necessary. And please remember that the act of practicing procedures is not something reserved for elementary students. Consider the fact that professional football teams practice the same procedures over and over and over, every day! Effective coaches, like effective teachers, recognize the importance of establishing and practicing procedures.

And here's another tip: Always pretend to assume, when students are not following a procedure, that they simply forgot the procedure. If you let them know that you think they are just being defiant by not following the procedure, then they are controlling you and will continue to do so. Instead, calmly say, "Oh, I see that a few of you have forgotten the procedure and need a little more practice." And then practice, like it's no big deal. Even if it IS a big deal to you, don't let them know that. Remain calm and simply practice the procedure with them again. If only one student continues to "forget" to follow a specific procedure, simply hold a private practice session with that student (see Tip 19).

Please remember that not all procedures can be established and practiced in one day. What you'll want to do is determine the most important procedures and practice those first. Once students are clear on those, add a few more. Just be careful not to overwhelm them with too many at a time because then you'll be inviting chaos and confusion – the opposite of what procedures are designed to accomplish.

✔ **Ask Yourself:** Do I have a list of procedures I expect my students to follow, have I determined which of those are of immediate importance, and am I establishing (and practicing) those procedures with my students on a consistent basis?

Tip 4
Minimize Discipline Problems

*In well-managed classrooms, discipline problems are few and far between
And the teachers appear happy, not disgruntled or mean.*

Often, the terms *discipline* and *classroom management* are mistakenly used synonymously. **Discipline is only one part of classroom management, albeit a vital one.** Your discipline plan (and you must have one) should consist of a set of a few rules. If a student breaks a rule, there is a definite consequence. This consequence is not contingent upon the frustration level of the teacher at the time the rule is broken, but rather is predetermined when the plan is being devised. Students are made aware of both the classroom rules and the consequences for not following those rules.

Rules are devised to set limits, to help maintain order, and to protect people. On our public highways, there are speed limits. If the limit is exceeded, there is a consequence: a speeding ticket. This consequence is predetermined. Motorists are aware of the consequences of exceeding the speed limit, just as students should be aware of the consequences of breaking rules in your classroom. Therefore, devise a discipline plan and enforce it consistently. And please ensure that your rules cover serious offenses only. Teachers often get into trouble, creating discipline problems, when they post 10, 15, 20 or so rules for the class, many of which relate to minor offenses. An example would be *talking*, which is procedural in nature. (For a practically foolproof way of getting students to stop talking out of turn, see Tip 19.) An example of a serious offense that would require a rule would be hitting others. Most teachers would agree that this is a serious offense, and that there should be a rule and consequence established to regulate this behavior.

Have you ever noticed that the very best teachers have very few discipline problems? The real key to their success does not lie in the way that they discipline their students after the rules have been broken. Rather, they have established ways of preventing most behavior problems through the structure of their classroom management plans along with their pleasant demeanors and proactive approaches to dealing with students. The simple fact is that in a well-managed environment there are very few discipline problems. The classroom hums like a well-rehearsed choir!

> ✔**Ask Yourself:** Have I determined a few (no more than five) rules to regulate serious offenses in my classroom, and are my students aware of the consequences of breaking those rules?

Tip 5
Use the "Are You All Right?" Technique

*Said the student to his teacher: "Once I believe you care
about me, I'll behave much better. Try it. You'll see!"*

The "Are You All Right?" technique is based on the simple premise that **students who believe you care about them are much more apt to behave.** It works like this: If a student is doing something inappropriate during class such as picking on others, talking excessively, refusing to do work, etc., simply step out into the hall with him or her and ask, "Are you all right?" with a sincere look of concern – not aggravation – on your face. Usually the student will answer, "Yes," with a look of disbelief. Then say, "Well, I'm asking because the way you were behaving was inappropriate and so unlike you." (Okay, so you're stretching the truth a little, because the way he was acting may have been quite typical …) Then say, "I knew, for you to be acting that way, something had to be bothering you, so I just wanted to know if you were all right and to let you know that if anything is bothering you, I'm here for you if you need to talk." That's it. You simply walk back into the classroom and resume teaching. And guess what happens! The student almost always abandons the misbehavior. And now you've accomplished several things: You've made the point that the behavior was inappropriate, you've maintained the student's dignity, you've acted out of concern instead of frustration, and you've let the student know that you care about him. What more could you want to accomplish?

But let's say that the student actually does have something bothering him, and he shares that with you when you ask if he is okay. Then listen to him. After you listen to what's bothering him, you say, "I can see how that would upset you. And I knew something had to be bothering you, because your behavior was inappropriate and so unlike you. Please know that you can come to me any time if you need to talk. Now let's get back to class." Prepare to be amazed at how well this simple technique works.

> ✔ **Ask Yourself:** Am I prepared to maintain my composure and use the "Are You All Right" technique, speaking privately with a misbehaving student and expressing my concern and willingness to listen and help?

Tip 6
Greet Students Daily

*When "I'm happy to see you" is what your face is telling,
students are more likely to buy the lessons you're selling!*

If you walk into Walmart, you will be greeted by someone you very likely do not know. This person's job is to welcome every customer who walks into the store. When you walk onto an airplane, you are greeted and welcomed. When you enter a restaurant, you are greeted, seated, and waited on. Why do these businesses spend so much money, time, and effort in ensuring that their patrons feel welcomed upon entering their places of business? The reason is that **people appreciate and respond positively to environments where they are made to feel welcomed and special.** The same holds true for the classroom. All too often, teachers are busy making last-minute preparations for class and do not stand at the door smiling and welcoming every student as they enter. Not greeting your students every day may be one of the biggest mistakes you could ever make.

So what does greeting students look like? There are actually three typical types of teacher greetings:

1. **The "gather the herd" greeting.** This is where the teacher stands at the door and rushes students into the class, saying things like, "Let's go, the bell's about to ring, get busy on your work as soon as you are seated, hurry." This type of greeting is much more like saying, "Welcome to my torture chamber." Avoid it at all costs.
2. **The "obligatorily cordial" greeting.** This is where the teacher stands at the door with possibly a half-baked smile as the students enter. There's nothing wrong with this greeting other than the fact that it doesn't really convince students you are happy to see them.
3. **The "I'm elated to see you" greeting.** This is where the teacher acts as though he or she is overjoyed to see the students by enthusiastically saying things like "How are you?" "Great to see you!" "I missed you when you were absent yesterday!" "Nice haircut!" "Thanks for coming to class." Yes, the teacher may be faking it just a tad or acting a little more enthusiastically than he or she feels on some days. Who cares, as long as the students don't know it. This is the kind of greeting that can

drastically reduce discipline problems. And it's FREE! It tells students you like them, you are happy to see them, you are in a good mood, and that they are in a welcoming environment. This is how you set the stage for success, *every* day, not just on your good days. Fake it if you must – and on some days you'll have to.

Students enjoy being in positive classrooms where they feel welcomed, and students succeed in positive environments. Happy, successful students? Any teacher will say "hello" to that!

✔ **Ask Yourself:** Do I want to maximize the chance of student success and minimize discipline problems *before* the students even enter my room each day? If your answer is yes, choose Greeting 3.

Tip 7
Learn What to Overlook

When the teacher looked for misbehavior in every cranny and nook,
the classroom became a chaotic place that the students overtook.

Kids are not perfect, and neither are adults. Teachers who expect perfect behavior from their students are being unrealistic and are inviting disappointment. For example, if you are expecting that your students will never whisper to one another, you've lost touch with reality. And if the occasional "whispering" is not overly distracting, overlook it. It's not a big deal. However, when many students begin talking and are off task, this should not be overlooked. The fact is that students will talk. They will make mistakes. They will act inappropriately at times. Why? Because they are children. Wise teachers know that if they get nit-picky about every little imperfection, they will literally run around putting out fires all day long, leaving little time for teaching.

The following are a few examples of behaviors that effective teachers tend to overlook:

- tapping a pencil on the desk
- quiet laughter between two students
- an occasional whisper from one student to another
- a student slouching in his desk
- a student attempting to push your buttons by talking to himself or making silly noises
- a student getting distracted for a brief period of time, etc.

There is no cookbook recipe listing exactly what can and cannot be overlooked in the classroom, but any behavior that is not impeding the learning of others and that will likely correct itself can usually be overlooked.

Another trick you might try is *tricking* the behavior away. If a student is talking to another student and you simply ask that student a question, he will stop talking to the other student. If a student seems distracted or bored, a simple change of activity will almost always correct the behavior. The key is to avoid giving annoying little behaviors any fuel. These behaviors usually aggravate the teacher more than they aggravate the rest of the students. Hide your aggravation behind your "blind eye" and your enthusiastic smile whenever possible.

> ✔ **Ask Yourself:** Do I tend to get nit-picky with behaviors I should overlook? Am I clear on what types of behaviors can and can't be overlooked? And am I willing to begin overlooking some of these annoying behaviors?

Tip 8
Handle Discipline Problems Discreetly

Reprove a student confidentially, and behavior will improve exponentially!

I call it the *Faculty Meeting Rule*, and it goes like this: **Do not say or do anything to your students in your classroom that you would not feel comfortable having your own principal say or do to you in a faculty meeting.** Wow! Imagine if all teachers treated all students the way these same teachers would expect to be treated by their own principals. The Faculty Meeting Rule serves as an excellent gauge, because just as teachers are among their peers in a faculty meeting and would not appreciate being singled out and embarrassed in front of their peers, students are among their peers in the classroom and the same holds true for them. Imagine how you would feel if your principal singled you out and reprimanded you publicly for talking to your neighbor during a faculty meeting. Most teachers would be mortified. Or how would you feel if the principal announced the results of each teacher's observations in the midst of everyone else? These are issues that should be discussed privately.

As teachers, we each have our own private "office." It's located right outside the classroom door, away from the rest of the students. Although it is not always possible to deal with every discipline challenge in total privacy, teachers should always use discretion. Discretion sometimes simply involves talking to a student at his desk in a quiet tone. Public reprimand simply does not work. It actually breeds resentment in students. Students will appreciate being treated with respect and will recognize that you value their privacy and dignity.

FACT: A student is much more likely to correct his misbehavior when his dignity has been maintained. Also, a student is not nearly as "tough" when you deal with him one on one, away from his *audience* (See Tip 19).

> ✔ **Ask Yourself:** When you are about to reprimand a student, quickly stop and ask yourself, "Would I be okay if my principal said this same thing to me in front of everyone in a faculty meeting?" If your answer is no, then you'll know not to say it to a student in front of his or her peers.

Tip 9
Handle Your Own Discipline Problems

Don't rely on administration
To handle every trial and tribulation,
Be in control of your own domain
And the students' respect you will certainly gain!

It is often said that **90 percent of a school's discipline referrals comes from 10 percent of the teachers.** Can it be that the 10 percent have all of the *problem* students? Not likely. What is more probable is that the remaining 90 percent of the teachers are handling their own discipline problems. They know that students respect teachers who are both capable of and willing to maintain a positive, active, and safe learning environment. They know that students respect teachers who are in control (not "controlling," but rather "in" control). This is not to say that effective teachers never have to refer student discipline problems to the office, but these occurrences are rare and are thus taken seriously by both the administration and the students. **Common misbehaviors such as talking, inattentiveness, attention seeking, teasing, etc. should be handled by the teacher.**

When a teacher sends a student to the office for a minor offense such as not turning in homework or failing to pay attention, the teacher is admitting to that student, to the rest of the students, and to the administration that he or she is not capable of handling typical classroom challenges. From here forward, the students know that they possess the power to control the teacher. This is the last thing you ever want your students thinking. Therefore, do what highly effective teachers do and, with only rare exceptions, handle your own discipline problems.

✔ **Ask Yourself:** Do I fall into the 90 percent of teachers who handle most of their own discipline problems? If not, what can I do to join that 90 percent?

Tip 10
Catch Students Behaving

A Little Praise

I helped a girl at school one day who had fallen and scraped her knee.
I only did what any kid would've done if he were me.
Then the teacher said that I was one of the nicest kids she'd met
And I thought to myself, "Well that's because she doesn't know me yet."
'Cause I'm really not so nice sometimes – I say and do bad things.
I don't always finish my homework or come in right when the bell rings.
But my teacher keeps on thinking that I'm really extra nice
So whenever I'm around her, I'm nice, not once, but twice.
I even work much harder when I am in her class.
Instead of going really slow, I finish extra fast.
She always takes the time to notice everything good I do.
She's told me I'm special so many times that I think it's becoming true.

Think back to your teacher training days and try to recall a course titled "How to Catch Students Behaving." Do you remember that course? No? That's because, as teachers, **we are trained to recognize problems, diagnose the causes of the problems, and then respond accordingly to solve these problems.** The ability to recognize and solve problems is a necessary skill that any effective teacher must possess. But how many of us were ever trained to recognize good behavior, diagnose what's causing the good behavior, and then foster that behavior so that it will continue? Not many. As teachers, we all have "eyes in the back of our heads" and can spot a child misbehaving from a mile away! Again, this is a good skill to possess. But an even more important skill is to be able to **use those same "eyes in the back of our head" to spot a child behaving well and encourage that good behavior or kind deed.** A simple acknowledgement of a positive behavior can work wonders.

Here are a few phrases you might use when "catching students behaving":

◆ Thanks for raising your hand.

◆ Thanks for remaining quiet while you wait for the others to finish.

◆ I appreciate the cooperation I'm observing from this group.

◆ Thanks for helping _____. That was very kind of you.

- I like the way you got to work so quickly.
- I noticed that you cleaned up around your work station. Thanks.

Uttering these types of positive phrases will soon become second nature to you. Students crave our attention, and they will usually do whatever it takes to get it. When they learn that they are much more apt to get our attention by behaving well, they begin behaving well. Teachers who focus more on *good* behavior than on *mis*behavior experience fewer discipline problems. So be on the look-out for good behavior. You'll begin to notice it everywhere!

✔ **Ask Yourself:** Do I make an effort, consistently, to spot good behavior and acknowledge it in order to foster even better behavior?

Tip 11
Be Proactive

Recognize what I'm about to do
And redirect my attention to you
And use clever ways to help me to
Never know that you knew what I was about to do!

Do you know what it looks like when students begin to get bored? When a student is upset? When a student is "thinking" about misbehaving? Anyone who has ever been around children or who has ever *been* a child can easily answer yes to all of these questions. And anyone who can answer yes to these questions can be proactive. **Being "proactive" simply means recognizing** *potential* **problems and stopping them before they become** *actual* **problems.**

Here is an example that epitomizes a teacher using a proactive approach to problem solving – or rather, problem preventing. I went to the door of a classroom one day to speak with a teacher. As we were speaking, she noticed that Tremain was out of his desk, heading toward Jonathon to hit him. The teacher immediately looked at him and said, "Tremain, thank you so much for going over to help Jonathon. I was just bragging to Ms. Breaux about how helpful you all are in this class, and there you are demonstrating it. Thank you, Tremain. I really appreciate your thoughtfulness." Tremain, caught totally off guard and completely distracted from his original *mission*, walked on over to Jonathon and helped him with his work. This, of course, was how the teacher handled every potential problem. She recognized it and immediately *broke the pattern of the student*. She turned the potentially negative situation around and cleverly managed to make it a positive one. If students were appearing bored, she changed the activity. When a student walked into class looking upset, she spoke to him privately, listened, and expressed concern. When a student was contemplating an inappropriate behavior, she often asked the student a question – completely unrelated to what was about to happen – in order to defuse the potential problem. Here's a quick example of that. A student is about to misbehave, and you say to the student, "Oh, remind me that I have to ask you about something later. Thanks." The fact that you have no idea what you will later ask the student is irrelevant. You simply wanted to stop the behavior that was about to occur.

The key is to spot the potential problem and redirect the student's attention in order to alter his behavior. It worked for this teacher, and it will work for you. Speaking of working, students work much harder and behave much better in the classrooms of proactive teachers.

> ✔ **Ask Yourself:** Do I know what it looks like when a student is about to misbehave, and do I attempt to redirect the student's attention *before* the misbehavior occurs?

Tip 12
Provide Frequent Stretch Breaks

Have you noticed how much pent-up energy students have as
they burst out of the school's doors at the end of the day?
Shouldn't they look a little more exhausted than they usually do?

Have you ever had to sit in a meeting for over an hour, or, better yet, an entire day? Have you gotten restless and/or bored? And have you noticed the talking that goes on between teachers during such meetings? Why is this? Basically, it's because teachers are active people. They are accustomed to moving around, *doing* things, and rarely sitting still during the day. The teachers walk out of the school building at the end of the day looking exhausted because they've been working all day long. So why is it that the students look so energetic? Could it be that they've been literally sitting most of the day? **FACT: Students are often off task or talking at inappropriate times because they are restless and in desperate need of some action.** What we need to see is the students looking exhausted at the end of the school day. Here is a simple, two-part way to make this happen:

1. **Become aware of the amount of time that your students are expected to remain seated during your classes.** Students need to be kept so busy that they don't have time to misbehave or be off task. This is not to say that the desks should be removed from the classrooms. Many classroom activities require students to be seated at their desks. But teachers who are aware of the energy just waiting to come out of those young bodies and minds use that awareness to their advantage.

2. **When you notice that students have been seated for more than thirty minutes or so (or even less for younger students), provide a stretch break.**

I recently observed a teacher who, out of nowhere it appeared, would say to the class, "Okay, when I say 'go,' you will have 45 seconds to stand up, stretch, and talk to your neighbors. Remember, however, that when I say 'stop,' you must be seated and quiet immediately." During a one-hour lesson, he did this three times. The students followed the procedure beautifully, and it appeared that they were accustomed to doing this. I also noted that the teaching activities moved quickly, the pace was steady, and the students remained on task throughout the lesson. Following the lesson, I asked the teacher about the frequent breaks. He smiled and said, "Oh, that. I don't know about you, but I know that I can't manage to sit still for more than 20 minutes at a time, and I'm much older than my students, so I don't have nearly the energy they do. I make it a practice to provide frequent stretch breaks. As you probably noticed, the breaks don't last long, but they work! I've also noticed that students are able to maintain more of a focus if they are allowed to stand up, stretch, and talk a little. It literally re-energizes them, and I need for my students to focus all the energy they have on what we're learning."

He went on to explain that even during times of active student participation involving group work, he still took time to give the students stretch breaks so that they could re-energize and refocus. "My students work hard in here," he said. "I want them to leave my classroom enlightened, inspired, and a little exhausted every day. If they don't, then I'm not doing my job."

✔ **Ask Yourself:** Do I provide time for students to stand up and stretch? If so, do I have a consistent procedure I use to make sure that the stretch break runs smoothly?

Tip 13
Use Proximity

The farther you stand from a student, the less likely he is to be prudent.

If someone were to ask your students, "Where does your teacher usually stand?" could they answer that question? Would they possibly point to a very distinct area, usually in the front of the classroom? If your answer is yes, read on.

A teacher once asked me, "Have you ever noticed that the 'problem' students always gravitate toward the back of the classroom? It never fails," he said. "My behavior problems, every year, come from the back of the room." Upon observing this teacher, I noticed that he never ventured past the front row of desks in the classroom. The farther back the students sat, the more they talked! Seated at the back of the room myself, I was almost tempted to join in the conversation, as I felt completely removed from both the teacher and the lesson. All the action was at the front of the room, so the students at the back created their own action. I also noticed that the only time the students at the back were acknowledged was with verbal reprimands or the *teacher eye* when the noise escalated. After the lesson, I asked the teacher if he would be willing to attempt an experiment in order to possibly alleviate the difficulties with his "problem" students. He agreed to participate. The experiment involved his use of proximity. For one week, I asked him to spend his teaching time moving around the classroom, spending time among all of the students. He also agreed that when a student was talking or was off task, he would calmly move closer to that student without the use of the *teacher eye* or verbal reprimands. One week later, I sat in the same classroom, but it definitely did not *feel* like the same classroom. Amazingly, the "problem" students were now actively involved in the lessons. Instead of talking to one another, they were involved in discussions with the teacher. And, not to my surprise, the teacher was noticeably more enthusiastic in his delivery. "I can't believe it," he said to me after the lesson. "How could I have missed that? I've been blaming the students during the five years I've been teaching. And the answer was so simple. I'm actually enjoying teaching now, and I can tell that the students are enjoying my lessons more."

The simple fact is that physical distance equates to mental distance in the classroom. If a student is off task, the simple act of standing closer to him will usually pull him right back into the lesson. And if you're constantly walking around the room as you teach, the very act of moving will help liven up the lesson. So get in there with your students. Be everywhere!

> ✔ **Ask Yourself:** Do I typically gravitate toward one or two areas of the classroom when I am teaching? If so, break that pattern and start moving around the room. Make the entire classroom your new comfort zone.

Tip 14
Do Not Provoke Defensiveness

Be Prepared for the Answer

If you're going to ask a question, be prepared for the answer
Or consider yourself a wooden floor where each student becomes a dancer.
They'll dance all over your question; they'll outsmart you every time
And you will end up treating them as if they've committed a crime.
So be careful about your questions; only ask what you want to know
And chances are better you'll be less of a fretter,
And your temper, you won't have to blow!

The following are actual teacher questions and the resulting student answers:

Teacher: How many times do I have to tell you?
Student: 6,284.
Teacher: Don't you have any home training?
Student: My dad is in jail, and my mom is on drugs!
Teacher: Do you want me to send you to the office?
Student: Actually, yes. It would be a nice break.
Teacher: Do you have a problem?
Student: No, but you look like you could use some anger management training!
Teacher: Don't you know this material?
Student: If I did, then I guess you'd be out of a job!

In all of the above scenarios, can you guess what the teachers' reactions were? The teachers were highly insulted. Although I am not, in any way, suggesting that the students' answers were appropriate, I am suggesting that these teachers *set themselves up* for the answers they received. These teachers were acting out of anger and frustration. In actuality, they were fueling the exact behaviors they were trying to diminish. The simple fact is that sarcastic questions provoke sarcastic answers. And, as we will discuss in Tip 84, there is no place for sarcasm in the classroom. If a student is struggling, instead of asking, "Do you have a problem?" in a sarcastic tone, simply say, "I notice

Section 1. Tip 14

Section One: Classroom Management ◆ 23

that you're struggling with this, and I'd like to help." Then do just that: assist the student. No sarcasm, no anger, no defensiveness. In the last question and answer above, the student actually made a very valid point: If students knew all the answers and exhibited perfect behavior and ample amounts of self-motivation, we would all be out of a job!

✔ **Ask Yourself:** Am I careful to prevent defensiveness in students, or do my questions or actions sometimes provoke it?

Tip 15
Avoid Down Time

Give a student nothing to do,
And he will find something to do, it's true.
But note that what he finds to do
Is usually not a task you want him to pursue!

Down time **consists of any time when a student has nothing to do.** When does down time typically occur in the classroom? It usually occurs when students finish an assignment early, when the teacher finishes a lesson before the end of the class period, or during transitions from one subject to the next. That's the problem, and here is the solution. Simply put, **the way to avoid down time is to structure every minute of the entire class period.** In other words, when giving an assignment, provide structured activities for early finishers. A note of caution here: Just because a student finishes early does not mean that he or she has completed the assignment correctly. Determine that first, and then you will know whether to provide enrichment activities or remediation activities at that point. Regardless, the student will keep busy either being enriched or remediated, but never just for the sake of keeping quiet. Next, do not make the mistake of under-planning where you may be left with several empty minutes at the end of the class period. When students have nothing to do, they'll find something to do, and it usually won't be to your liking! Therefore, **teach from "bell to bell."**

Regarding transitions, implement structured procedures that make the transitions smooth and efficient. My favorite example comes from my own classroom experiences. I noted that during transitions, where I would instruct the students to put one set of materials away and prepare for the next subject, it was inevitable that the following would occur: Some students would be ready to go in seconds, some would be seated on the floor looking inside their desks, some would start cleaning the insides of their desks, some would engage in conversations with others, and so on. This was eating away valuable teaching and learning time. So I began to do the following, which has continued to work wonders for me and for countless others with whom I have shared the technique – and it works with all age levels. I discovered that students enjoy being "timed" during transitions, and I used that discovery to implement a procedure. I would say, "Okay, don't move until I say 'go.' But when I say 'go,' I want you to pick up your reading books and get out your language projects from yesterday. I'm going to be timing you, and the world record for seventh graders is 9.243 seconds. (Of course, I was just fabricating this!) When you're ready to go, give me a 'thumbs up.' And when all thumbs are up, I'll record your time. Go!" Amazingly, it worked! Within seconds, all students were ready to go and anxious to see if they had set the new world record. Even more amazingly, I would hit my watch when I said 'go' and hit it again when all thumbs were up. Then I would say something like, "Wow! You did that in 8.987 seconds. You've got the new world record!" I was just wearing a plain old watch – not a stopwatch – and the students never figured that out! They even began competing with my other classes to see if they could beat one another's times. They had me keep charts on the wall so that they could compare their times with my other classes. And they never tired of it!

Question: **Why did the students never tire of this procedure?** You'll probably be tempted to think that the answer lies in the competition or the fun nature of the activity. Good guesses, but wrong. There's only one reason the students never tired of it: MY ENTHUSIASM! Every day, for every transition, I pretended I couldn't wait to see if they could beat their previous times. My excitement became theirs! Oh, and if I ever had (and I did) one student who did not participate in the activity, I pretended not to notice. Pick your battles carefully. Over the years, I have personally proven that the technique works at ALL grade levels. So give it a try. It's great fun, students enjoy it, it adds excitement, and it saves time and aggravation. The record set by my class was 5.3245678932 seconds. I challenge you to beat that!

✔ **Ask Yourself:** Do I structure each class period to avoid down time? And do I have a procedure in place to help ensure that transitions are smooth and quick?

Tip 16
Put Students at Ease

When, with negativity, the classroom is whirring
Very little, if any, learning is occurring.

Research has shown, time and again, that when we are feeling anxious or nervous, our brains begin to focus solely on ways to relieve the anxiety. Research also shows that **our brains take much longer to process a negative statement than to process a positive statement.** Did we even need research to tell us that? Just think about it. When you're upset about something, it becomes your focus because you want to feel better. Not exactly rocket science! Now consider this one. If someone said, "Your hair looks nice today," you would probably thank the person and move on. It would feel nice to receive the compliment, but the compliment would not overtake your thinking. Conversely, if someone said, "Whatever look you were going for with your hair today, you missed!" you would most likely, after checking your hair in the mirror, feel upset. Then you would begin trying to figure out why they said what they said. You may even begin to experience a little righteous indignation. You might get angry, and anger sometimes leads to retaliation. But the fact is that no matter how hard you would try to let it go, your brain would want to focus on it for a while. It's a lot tougher to just *move on* when someone says something negative about you than it is when someone says something positive about you.

So what are the ramifications of this in the classroom? Again, it doesn't take a rocket scientist to understand that **in a negative environment – one where students are fearful, uncomfortable, and anxious – very little learning can take place** because all of those young brains are too busy focusing on trying to feel LESS fearful, LESS uncomfortable, and LESS anxious. You, the teacher, can *nip this one in the bud* very easily and very early on. Here's how to do it. On the very first day of school, make it your number one priority to put your students at ease. Display a calm, composed demeanor. Make everything about you and your classroom say, "Welcome! I'm glad you're here." And then do one of the most important things you will do all year: Make promises to your students. **When you introduce** yourself, begin NOT by telling them what you expect of them, but what *they* can expect of *you*. Tell them about how exciting your class will be. Then make the following two promises to them:

1. **I will never raise my voice in this classroom.** That's right. I will not yell at you. That is not to say that I won't deal with misbehavior and hold you accountable, because I will. But I promise that I will deal with you in a private manner and treat each of you with respect. (Oh, and you don't have to add, "And I'll expect you to treat me with respect also," because students will automatically treat you with respect once they know you respect them.)
2. **I will never intentionally embarrass you in front of your peers.** So relax. You're safe here, and you're going to be amazed at how much we're all going to learn this year!

By making these two promises, you have accomplished two things:

1. **You have just made yourself accountable to your students.** Who better to hold you accountable? In case you don't yet know this, students will "hold you to your promises." And you'll lose their trust if you ever break a promise. So, basically, you've just taken the option of *losing your cool* away from yourself.
2. **You have managed to put your students at ease.** When students are at ease, they will do their best; they will accept challenges; they will behave; they will succeed; and, most importantly, they will never forget you for it!

> ✔ **Ask Yourself:** Do I make every effort to put my students at ease as opposed to on edge?

Tip 17
Provide Structured "Bell-work"

When you keep your students engaged and active,
they can't find the time for behavior that's distractive!

Why is it that some classrooms become chaotic as soon as the students enter? And why is it that, in other classrooms, students enter and begin working immediately? The simple answer is that **effective teachers know that they must have structured bell-work awaiting the students each day as they enter the classroom.** What is bell-work? Bell-work (also called lesson starters, bellringers, and other terms) is an assignment that is posted in the same place every day for students to begin as soon as they walk into the room. The assignment is brief and interesting to the students, and it relates to the lesson that will be taught that day. Let's say that you will be discussing our country's justice system for the day's lesson. For the daily bell-work, you might have the following assignment posted:

> *Pretend that as of today, there are no more school rules. All students are free to do what they wish, with no limitations. Think about this for a minute, and then write three examples of realistic situations that could occur as a result of having no rules. Then, list three reasons you believe that rules are/are not necessary in this school.*

This bell-work assignment would take only a few minutes and would lead into a discussion of societal rules, laws, consequences, etc.

One of the keys to successful classroom management is to keep students *so busy they're dizzy* from the moment they walk into the classroom until the moment they leave. Before they know it, class is over. Where did the time go? That's how students feel when they remain actively and meaningfully engaged in their learning. And that active and meaningful learning begins with a structured bell-work assignment at the beginning of each class period.

✔**Ask Yourself:** Do I have a quick, meaningful activity for students to get started on as soon as they enter the class each day? And is this activity posted in the same place every day so that students know exactly where to find it?

Tip 18
Avoid Power Struggles with Students

If I Could

If I could, then I would, whether or not you think I should.
I wouldn't because I couldn't; not because you think I shouldn't.
But I can't, so I won't, and since I won't then I don't.
Now should you feel confused, or should you feel amused?
Since you won't tell me what I should, then I won't tell you, but I could!

Effective teachers do not engage in power struggles with students, period. I was observing a teacher's class when one of the students strutted in and announced, "Guess what! My daddy won the lottery last night, and he said I can quit school, so good riddance to all of you!" I have to admit that I was amazed when the teacher simply looked at him, smiled, and said, "Boy, aren't you lucky!" and she immediately began teaching. The student had no *come-back* because he, too, was amazed and, I suppose, a little shocked. He simply went to his seat. I am quite certain that the student was attempting to provoke a struggle. However, it takes two people, and one wasn't playing. The teacher did not react, nor did she attack.

Now consider the same scenario in the classroom of a teacher who engages in power struggles with students. It would have gone something like this:

Student: Guess what! My daddy won the lottery last night, and he said I could quit school, so good riddance to all of you!

Teacher: First of all, young man, your father did not win the lottery because we would have heard about it. Also, you're not old enough to quit school. Don't ever come barging into my classroom like that again!

Can you imagine where this could lead? Instead of engaging in power struggles with students, effective teachers **defuse the situation immediately by not providing the student with the desired response.** Quite simply, they do not add fuel to the fire.

✔ **Ask Yourself:** Do I ever find myself battling with a student for power or control? Remember that you always have a choice. You can choose to engage in a power struggle with a student or you can choose to defuse the misbehavior. CHOOSE to DEFUSE!

Tip 19
Hold Private Practice Sessions

To my teacher: Please use discretion with me
rather than aggression with me,
and please have a private session with me
when you discuss my behavior transgression with me!

FACT: If you deal with a student's misbehavior in front of the class, the behavior will rarely improve. It may even worsen, because the student will have an *audience*. But when you deal with students privately, even the toughest of students are suddenly not so tough. The following strategy is practically magic. You will be amazed at its positive results.

Let's say that a student is a chronic talker. Simply talk to the student privately and say, "I noticed that you're having trouble remembering our procedure for raising your hand before speaking. Don't be too hard on yourself. I forget things, too. But I know how embarrassing it can be to forget so often in front of your friends, so I'll do a favor for you. I'll give you my recess today and I'll practice that procedure with you so that you'll get better at it and won't forget so much. I'm happy to do that for you. See you at recess." That's it. What you're doing is pretending to think that the student is simply forgetting to raise his hand. Surely he would not be ignoring the procedure purposefully! The key is that you are not at all sarcastic and that you tell him that you are giving of your own time to help him. So instead of taking his recess from him, you're giving him yours!

So the student comes in at recess and you say, "Thanks for coming in. Now pretend that you are in class and you have something to say. Show me what you will do." The student raises his hand, and you say, "Great! I can give you 15 more minutes of practice. Do you need more practice or do you think you have it?" The student always says, "I have it." Then say, "Great. See you tomorrow. Oh, and if you forget again, that's my fault. It simply means I didn't give you enough practice time. I'll even stay after school if you need. Just let me know."

Please note that the technique takes less than a minute, so you will not lose your recess. And if you teach in a school where there is no recess, you can use this quick technique between classes, during your planning period, during lunchtime, etc. You'll be amazed at the results if you use this technique appropriately. But if your approach even hints at sarcasm, it will not work.

When the student next returns to your class, be sure to catch him when he is *not* talking and thank him. If the problem ever becomes chronic again, simply hold another private practice session. You can use this for practically any sort of misbehavior. The *private practice session* strategy is a simple one that produces astonishing results at all grade levels.

> ✔ **Ask Yourself:** Am I committed to dealing with student misbehavior privately whenever possible?

Tip from Breaux, A. and Whitaker, T. (2010). *50 Ways to Improve Student Behavior*. New York, NY: Routledge.

Tip 20
Make the Punishment Fit the Misbehavior

FACT: Logical consequences breed logical results!
Illogical consequences breed illogical results!

I once watched a teacher punish a student who was talking out of turn. The punishment consisted of writing the entire text that he was supposed to be reading at the time of the misbehavior. I then thought to myself, "Wait a minute. This is a language arts teacher. Isn't she supposed to be instilling a love of reading and writing in these students? But isn't this punishment making the act of writing seem tedious, boring, and punitive? Isn't this particular punishment fostering more a loathing than a love of reading and writing?" There was no logic to this punishment. Following the lesson, I asked her about her choice of punishment and her desired result. She answered, "Well, I wanted him to pay attention and to stop talking out of turn." "Did it work?" I asked. "No, not at all. He became quite defensive and refused to do the work. He threw his pencil aside and said he couldn't write all of that. Then he began talking again." "Why did you choose this particular punishment?" I asked. "I didn't know what else to do. His talking was aggravating me, so I just said the first thing that came to my mind." My suggestion to her was to try to make the punishment fit the misbehavior next time. She decided that a logical response to the misbehavior might have been to talk to him privately and let him know that his behavior was inappropriate and distracting to the other students. As a consequence, he would not be allowed to talk during the break between subjects, where students were allowed one minute of talking/stretching time.

The above scenario is a common one. **Teachers get frustrated, and they dole out illogical consequences**, saying things like, "If you don't stop it, you'll never see another recess." Or better yet, they make students write something like, "I will not talk out of turn" several hundred times. Where's the logic in that? There is none. Can you imagine being pulled over by a policeman who has had a frustrating day and decides to take your car away for a year as a punishment for having a broken headlight? Or can you imagine being caught doing what all teachers do – talking during a faculty meeting – and having to write, "I will not talk during faculty meetings" 500 times? These consequences are not logical, and they would only breed resentment.

You do not want to breed resentment in students. Rather, you want to instill in them that rules are rules and they exist for a reason. If they choose to break a rule, then a consequence will follow – a *logical* one.

> ✔ **Ask Yourself:** Do I resist the temptation to let my frustration determine a punishment and its duration?
> And do I make it clear that there's a consequence to an action, and that a logical consequence will follow an infraction?

Tip 21
Attack the Problem, Not the Person

If you don't attack the problem and instead attack the person,
the problem with that person will definitely worsen!

One of the biggest mistakes a teacher can make is to confuse the problem with the person. The two must be separated in order to truly deal with any problem or any person effectively. Let's make the concept simple. A student is consistently failing tests. You know that this student is quite capable. Attacking the person might sound like this: "Rebecca, I know you're capable, so you need to start putting forth some effort and paying attention in class. You should be making As, but instead you're making Fs. What's the matter with you?" Notice the sarcasm in the teacher's words and the blame placed upon the person. Also notice that the teacher, unaware of the cause of the problem, poses a *solution* for the student. Now let's consider the same scenario where the teacher attacks the problem instead of the person: "Rebecca, I notice that you're struggling with your grades. Knowing how capable you are, I'm concerned and was wondering if you could shed some light on what's going on. You seem to be distracted from your studies. Maybe I can help." Do you see the difference in the approach? Do you see how, in this scenario, the student's dignity is maintained, as the focus is on the problem and not the person? **It is human nature to defend against personal attack, and students are definitely human.** So the first scenario would likely lead to a defensive attitude from the student as opposed to a solution to the problem.

One teacher summarized it quite well after I witnessed an interesting encounter she had with a student. The student walked into class very upset about something that had happened on the playground. She immediately began picking on another student in the classroom. The teacher asked her to be seated and the student retaliated with, "Leave me alone, you_____" (I'm sure you can fill in the expletive). The teacher very calmly whispered something to the student, the student sat down, and the teacher began teaching, as if nothing had happened. After she got the class busy, she walked out with the student and had a private discussion. Following class, I said, "I was impressed with how calmly you handled that situation. I'm also curious as to what it was you said when you whispered to her and calmed her down." The teacher smiled and said, "Well, this student just moved here. So she doesn't know me well enough yet to determine whether I am a _____ or not. I may be, and I may not be, but she'll have to get to know me better before she can make such a statement. So I simply leaned over and explained what I just said to you. I told her that I would give her a few minutes to regain her composure and then we would deal with what had just happened. And of course, we did deal with it, and I learned a lot about that student in a little bit of time." I then asked, "Do you always handle such situations this calmly and professionally?" Once again, the teacher smiled and said, "I believe that if we, as teachers, really knew the faces behind the masks of some students, and if we understood what caused them to behave so inappropriately at times, and if we had any idea what struggles some of these students face, what cumbersome emotional loads some of them are carrying, then we would be heartbroken instead of angry." She followed that by saying, "Please understand that I don't excuse their behaviors. But my attitude and the beliefs that I just shared with you enable me to attack the problem instead of the person. I love my students, and whether they accept that love or not, I keep loving them anyway. Sooner or later, they all come around when they realize that I do care and that I won't attack."

✔ **Ask Yourself:** When a student misbehaves, am I careful to deal with the problem while maintaining the student's dignity? Am I clear that I care about the student and want to help him solve his problem as opposed to acting angry with the student for even having a problem?

Tip 22
Start Over on ANY Day!

**One of the perks of teaching is that we get
to start over every day, not just every year.**

A new teacher said to me, "I've lost control of the students. But it's the middle of the school year. Isn't it too late to start over?" My answer to her and my answer to you is that though it is easier if you have established and maintained control from the first day of school than it is to *regain* control once it has been lost, it is never too late to start over. We can start afresh tomorrow.

The following is a little *trick* for starting over on any day. Whenever you want to try something new – due to the fact that what you were doing was not working – use the *teacher meeting* trick. It goes like this:

Let's say that students are talking out of turn a lot, and the behavior is getting worse. Instead of saying, "You've gotten out of control with your talking, so I'm going to start punishing you from today on if you talk out of turn," simply say, "I attended a teacher meeting and we were discussing sixth-grade procedures. I know you're only fifth graders, but I told the teachers at the meeting that my fifth graders could handle this procedure. Would you like to try it?" They always agree, and then you set your new procedure for talking. You practice it and make them successful and praise them, and then you practice and make them successful and praise them, over and over. Then you say, "Wow, I can't wait to tell everyone at the next teacher meeting that you all are able to handle sixth-grade procedures! I'm so proud of you."

Now you've established a new procedure. Just follow through and be consistent, and continue to set students up for success. If one student is not following the procedure, use the *private practice session* we discussed in Tip 19. You can use the *teacher meeting* trick for any grade level, by the way. You can use it to regain control, or you can use it to establish new procedures. And your students think you attend weekly teacher meetings, so you appear super-dedicated!

Usually, when teachers lose control of management or when procedures do not work, it reflects a lack of consistency on the part of the teacher.

So establish your procedures, be consistent in implementing them, and remain in control of yourself, first and foremost, so that you won't lose control of your students.

> ✔ **Ask Yourself:** Do I tend to waste time fretting over past mistakes or failed attempts at maintaining control? If so, simply analyze what did not work, learn from it, and start over today!

Classroom Management: Section Highlights

- Make a positive first impression by welcoming students with smiles, enthusiasm, and promises of an exciting, successful school year.
- Establish a clear, concise classroom management plan and implement it consistently.
- Tell students what you expect, show them how to meet those expectations, and practice procedures with them until those procedures become routines.
- Remember that students work harder and behave better when they believe you genuinely care about them.
- Greet students daily as if you are elated to see them.
- Avoid being nit-picky: Ignore minor aggravations or behaviors that can be overlooked.
- Never say or do anything to a student in front of his or her peers that you would not feel comfortable having your principal say or do to you in a faculty meeting.
- Avoid sending students to the office. Whenever possible, handle your own discipline problems.
- Catch students behaving in order to foster even better behavior.
- Recognize when a problem is about to occur, and use proactive measures to stop it from occurring.
- Provide quick stretch breaks in order to re-energize and refocus students.
- Move throughout the room as you teach. Be everywhere!
- Keep students busy from bell to bell.
- Create a positive, non-threatening, welcoming environment in order to promote optimal learning and behavior.
- Don't allow yourself to engage in power struggles with students.
- Hold private practice sessions with students to deal with behavior infractions.
- Ensure that consequences for broken rules are logical ones.
- Attack the problem behind the person, not the person behind the problem.
- When something stops working, let it go, reassess, and start over.

Section Two

Planning

The Rewards of Planning

Coaches go into every game with a very specific plan
And surgeons plan their surgeries and proceed with a steady hand.
Attorneys defend their clients following much preparation
And players of chess only make a move after much deliberation.
Travelers go on vacation with their maps and proper clothing,
So why is it that some teachers speak of lesson plans with loathing?
The fact remains that failing to plan becomes a plan to fail.
You're a ship without an anchor, a hammer without a nail.
So plan your lessons every day,
Stay on the path so you won't go astray,
Know why you're teaching the things that you teach,
And reap your rewards from the students you reach.

Tip 23
Manage Your Time Wisely

*There's only so much time in the day, and not enough time to do it all.
There's no way to finish all I have to do. What is sleep? I can't recall . . .*

A new teacher came into my office in tears one day, saying, "I just can't do this. There aren't enough hours in the day." "Aren't enough hours in the day to do what?" I asked. "To be a teacher and still have a life – to grade papers, plan lessons, complete other paperwork, and still manage to take care of my family at home. It's just not possible. I think I've chosen the wrong profession. My family is also beginning to suffer, because all I do is schoolwork, and I can't allow that to continue." So I asked her to map out her day for me – her typical routine. It went like this:

- Wake up, and either grade a paper or two or spend a few minutes planning.
- Prepare breakfast, and try to grade another paper or two while eating.
- Get ready for school and get my child ready.
- Arrive at school, get a little more work done – usually while visiting with co-workers.
- Teach all day – with one hour of planning time, usually spent listening to the gripes of co-workers.
- Come home from school and spend all afternoon and evening trying to juggle cooking, cleaning, grading, planning lessons, doing homework with my child, etc.
- Spend time on my cell phone and on social media sites getting caught up with friends and family.
- Cry myself to sleep in the wee hours of the morning!

I knew I had to help this teacher to develop some time management skills. What she was doing was running from one activity to the next, never really finishing one before she moved on to another. It would be overwhelming for any teacher to try to accomplish what she was attempting on such a schedule. So I made a simple suggestion that literally changed her life. I asked her how much focused time she had set aside every day to be completely alone with planning and paperwork – completely removed from her cell phone, her friends on social media sites, etc. The answer, as you saw from her schedule, was none. I then asked if it would be possible to either come to school one hour earlier or stay one hour later – ALONE – in her classroom, focusing only on the task at hand, not multi-tasking while tweeting, pinning, posting, blogging, etc. She said she could come one hour earlier, because her husband took her child to school in the mornings. So we agreed that she would commit to one hour, every morning, of uninterrupted planning time. We also *found* another hour during the day: her planning period. (Remember that her planning period was not being used for actual planning.) She agreed that instead of going into the teachers' lounge, listening to and engaging in conversations with others, she would now spend that time in her room, alone. She agreed that she could socialize with her co-workers during recess and lunchtime.

The results? I received a phone call from the teacher. She said, "You saved my life! I'm sticking to my schedule, and it's working. I don't even have to take work home with me anymore. I have my life back. And I'm managing to stay on top of my planning, grading, and paperwork." She added, "Oh, and both my students and my family have noticed that I'm a much nicer and happier person!"

✔**Ask Yourself:** How much time do I set aside each day for uninterrupted planning and grading – away from any distractions – just me, focusing on my students?

Tip 24
Understand That Teaching is Hard Work

*We work so hard for an "income" that's nominal
But the final reward – the "outcome" – is phenomenal!*

"Oh, you're a teacher? Aren't you lucky! You get weekends off and tons of holidays and months of vacation in the summers. Wait, what time do you finish teaching every day? Wow! You've got it made!" Have you heard that yet? If not, you will. And when you do, I can guarantee you that whoever says it has never been a teacher! What people (who are not teachers) will never understand – so don't try to explain it, please – is that teaching is possibly the most demanding of all professions. It is also the most noble and rewarding!

Regrettably, many new teachers enter the profession with no concept of what will be required of them. They are often shocked to learn of all the paperwork and planning time involved, all the skills that are required to teach and manage a classroom effectively, all the patience, understanding, and empathy they must possess, all the many hats they must wear, all the problems some students bring to school with them. . .

Please understand that teaching is hard work! The road will be rocky at times. You will stumble and fall on occasion. You may even bleed a little. But remember that nothing worthwhile comes easily. The rewards of teaching far outweigh the demands. You will know this the first time you make a student smile, the first time you receive a sweaty hug, the first time you dry a student's tears on your shirt sleeve, the first time you open a present with crinkled wrapping paper and way too much tape, and any time you witness the slightest or greatest of achievements and the least or greatest of efforts from the students whose very lives you are helping to shape.

Yes, teaching is hard work. And the title *Teacher* is reserved only for those willing to rise to its many challenges, to give of themselves completely, and to be humble enough to accept (with dignity, grace, and resolute determination) its tremendous responsibilities. If you are reading this, then you are very likely one of those chosen few.

> ✔ **Ask Yourself:** Am I aware that teaching is going to challenge me by requiring hard work, dedication, and immense responsibility? And am I committed to accepting those challenges?

Tip 25
Put Off Procrastinating

I'll Do it Tomorrow

I didn't feel like doing it, so I put it off for a day
And the next day came and I put off more – too much was coming my way.
I used up tons of paper with my list of "things to do"
And every day my "list of things" just grew and grew and grew.
It overtook my kitchen, then it overtook my house.
It overtook my children and it overtook my spouse.
If only I had done the things that needed to be done,
It would have been much easier to do things one by one.
But now I'm overwhelmed with all the things I did not do.
How will I survive this? I do not have a clue!
And sitting atop these things to do are feelings of guilt and sorrow,
So I'm turning over a new leaf. Yep, I'll do it tomorrow!

It happens to new teachers (and veteran teachers) all the time – they enter the "I'll do it tomorrow" cave. I call it a cave because it is a dark and scary place to live! Do NOT – I repeat – Do NOT go in there! It is alluring, I know. We all experience being overwhelmed from time to time, and it's easy to put one thing off. Then two things. Then three. And soon enough, you're swallowed by all you have to do, and there is no end in sight. It's that old familiar feeling of cramming for an exam the night before when you could have taken the smart route by studying over time, a little at a time. At least you could have passed the exam that way without a mental breakdown. I simply cannot stress enough how important it is that you, as a new teacher, do not allow yourself to procrastinate. It's much better to be on top of your workload than to have your workload on top of you!

✔**Ask Yourself:** Do I tend to put things off until the last minute? Have I fallen behind on paperwork, lesson planning, etc.? If so, what steps can I take to begin staying ahead of (or at least keeping in step with) my workload?

Tip 26
Plan Effective Lessons

If you plan your lessons with careful attention
And treat each one as a special invention
You're sure to see student success and retention
Reducing your levels of stress and tension!

The very best teachers know that **if you want to *have* a great lesson, you have to *plan* a great lesson**. It truly is that simple. But understand that planning takes time. However, if you teach a well-planned lesson, then you can really enjoy your teaching. Now, does that mean that you will accomplish everything you intend to accomplish or that your plan will go off without a hitch? Of course not. Teaching is not an exact science, and that is why we need to plan so thoroughly.

Teachers who do not plan good lessons end up struggling with behavior problems, off-task students, and general chaos. In order for the students to learn a new skill, the lesson must be well thought-out and well taught. Good planning is a skill; and it requires training, patience, practice, and guidance. Mentors can play a critical role by spending time planning with new teachers.

The following are some simple tips for you to use when planning any lesson:

- ◆ Determine your objective.
- ◆ Decide how you will make the lesson interesting and inviting for your students.
- ◆ Be sure to make an effort to actively involve your students in every part of the lesson.
- ◆ Plan to state the lesson's purpose, relate the skill to students' real lives, teach and model the skill, practice the skill with them, have them try the new skill independently, and review. This approach may be applied to any new curriculum or standards that come along.
- ◆ Gather any necessary materials beforehand.
- ◆ Enjoy teaching your well-planned lesson!

> ✔**Ask Yourself:** Do I plan all lessons and activities following the aforementioned steps? If so, you should see instant (and positive) results from your students.

Tip from Breaux, A. and Whitaker, T. (2015). *Seven Simple Secrets: What the BEST Teachers Know and Do! 2nd edition.* New York: Routledge.

Tip 27
Be Organized and Prepared

Organizing is what you do before you do something, so that when you do it, it is not all mixed up.

—A.A. Milne

Organization is not a skill that comes naturally or easily to some. However, it is a skill that MUST be acquired if you desire to be an effective teacher. An organized room gives the message that the teacher is competent and well prepared. And **in organized environments, students tend to be more organized, more respectful of the classroom property, more respectful of the teacher, and better behaved.** Students want and need structure. They want a teacher who is well prepared and well organized. Knowing where everything is – a place for everything, and everything in its place – makes for a calmer environment. I have often noticed that when classrooms are in disarray and the teacher is running from here to there trying to locate materials during the lesson or trying to fill in with something to keep the students busy, the students tend to mimic that behavior.

The bottom line is this: If your classroom is an ordered, highly functional place, the students will be much more likely to mimic that order. And when teachers are organized and prepared, there is very little, if any, time for off-task behavior. The class runs smoothly from bell to bell. Procedures are established, materials are readily available, the room is not cluttered or dirty, the lessons flow smoothly, and the whole environment is that of a safe, orderly, inviting place to learn.

Now let's look at the other side of that scenario. I walked into a teacher's classroom some time back, and I couldn't believe my eyes. There was *stuff* everywhere. Student projects were all over the floor, the desks just seemed to be scattered around, there were stacks of books and papers everywhere, the teacher's desk looked like it had been struck by a tornado, and there was garbage that *hadn't quite made it* lying beside the garbage can. The teacher, flustered, was literally running between activities trying to find this worksheet or that lesson plan or some textbook. The students were out of their desks, talking, roaming about. One student actually tripped on one of many obstructions in the aisle. For one solid hour, I witnessed no actual teaching and learning. Everyone just sort of blended in with the mess. In one word: chaos. The teacher apologized for the mess and jokingly said, "The custodian won't even come in here to clean." Needless to say, we saw to it that she received some guidance from her mentor and from a few other willing teachers who agreed to spend part of a Saturday helping her to get organized. Although things are not completely in order yet, she has come a long way. A visit to her classroom after she became better organized revealed the following:

- Teaching and learning taking place.
- Better student behavior.
- Better student participation.
- Much less off-task behavior.
- A calmer environment.
- A more positive environment.

Students need and deserve structured, ordered, welcoming environments. Disarray keeps learning away!

✔**Ask Yourself:** Would my students describe me as an organized teacher – one who is always prepared and who structures the class so that lessons flow, everyone is engaged and busy, and no one's life is at risk amid clutter and chaos?

Tip 28
Maintain Accurate Records

Maintain accurate documentation
To lessen your own and your students' frustration
And don't just collect it, but use the information
To help in your lesson and strategy formation.

What benefits are there for students if a teacher maintains accurate records? The benefits are simple: Improved teaching and learning! I was called into a school to help deal with a "problem" student. The student had two teachers, only one of whom was having difficulties with him, so I decided to acquire input from both. When I spoke with the first teacher and asked her to tell me about Thomas, she went to her computer and pulled up his grades. Next to Thomas's name were all failing grades. I then asked the teacher to tell me about Thomas's strengths. She responded, "He has no real strengths, as you can see from his grades." "What does he struggle with most?" I asked. "Everything," she responded. "He won't behave, and he refuses to put any effort into his schoolwork." I asked if she had work samples, behavior records, documentation of anything she was doing to improve the situation, etc. The only things she could produce were several test papers with big fat red Fs on them – no comments, nothing. I then asked what types of unique approaches she was taking or strategies she was using to accommodate his specific needs. Once again, she could give me nothing. I thought to myself, "How can you accommodate a student's needs if you don't even know what his needs are?" There was no doubt in my mind as to why Thomas was *drowning* in this teacher's classroom. I then moved on to the next teacher. Thomas's grades in her class were much better. She also showed me a portfolio of his work, letters of communication with his father, a picture of him on a bulletin board, a letter he had written to her, a chart on his behavior, samples of graded assignments on which she had written lots of comments (most of which were positive, and all of which were constructive). And last, but definitely not least, there were teacher notes that specified unique approaches and strategies she used to teach Thomas, with red asterisks next to those that were the most successful. Not surprisingly, Thomas, though not making straight As, posed no problems academically or behaviorally in this teacher's classroom. She went on to tell me, without my asking, about all of Thomas's strengths: his outgoing personality, his leadership qualities, his creativity, and his determination to succeed, especially when things did not come easily to him. Was this the same Thomas? Yes, but I would never have known it by listening to the two "eye witness" accounts! Same Thomas, different teachers. You decide.

Bottom line: **Effective teachers maintain accurate records in order to track student progress, to identify patterns in student learning and behavior, to adjust teaching accordingly, and to communicate effectively with parents.** Needless to say, the lives of all the "Thomases" are profoundly affected.

✔**Ask Yourself:** Do I maintain accurate records for the sake of improving teaching and student achievement? And do I provide parents with updated and accurate information to keep them abreast of each student's progress, strengths, and struggles?

Tip 29
Make the Objectives Clear for Each Lesson

Having no destination creates a sticky situation
For you'll never know when you get there; you could be there right now . . .
But where is "there" when you're not aware? Confusing, bemusing? And how!

"What did you learn in school today?" ask many parents when their kids
return home. "I don't know," answer far too many children. "Well, what did
you do?" ask the parents. "Well, we had to write a lot and read some stories
and do some math problems and read a chapter and answer the questions
at the end of the chapter and fill out a lot of stupid worksheets!" Okay, so
now we know what they did, but we still don't know what they learned or
if they actually learned anything at all. Now, if a student comes home and
says, "I learned how to figure out the square footage of our classroom and I
learned how to identify opposing viewpoints in an article and we compared
the voting process in three other countries to our own voting process," then
you know exactly what they have learned!

Imagine going on a vacation and having no destination. How would
you know what to pack? Imagine a doctor performing surgery without an
objective. "Oh well, I'll just open him up and take a look around and see
what's what!" Or imagine being the patient, knowing you'll be undergoing
surgery, but you have no idea why! I know, it seems ridiculous. But it's just
as ridiculous for students to be unclear on exactly what it is they're supposed
to be accomplishing in the classroom every day.

Simply stated, **an objective defines what the students should know or
be able to do at the end of each lesson**. I've often watched teachers tell
students to read a chapter and answer the questions at the end of the chapter
when they're finished. The students reluctantly get busy, but they have no
idea _why_ they have to do this. In fact, it's a good rule to know that when
students ask, "Why do we have to do this?" it's like a red flag reminding you
that you have obviously forgotten to make the objective for the lesson clear.
It goes without saying that you, the teacher, must write clear, measurable
objectives for every lesson you teach. But that's not enough. You must now
make the objectives clear to your students. Make it a point, as you begin each
lesson, to tell your students, "Guess what you'll be able to do at the end of
this lesson," and then tell them. And as you're engaging your students in

learning activities, make sure they know what they're doing and why they're doing it. Then, as you review with the students, have them tell and show you what they have learned. But first, YOU must know what you want the students to know and/or do, why you want them to know it or do it, and how you will get them there.

> ✔**Ask Yourself:** Are my students aware, every day, of what they are learning and why they are learning it? And when they leave my classroom, could they tell someone exactly what they learned in my class today?

Tip 30
Provide a Plan for Substitutes

Students can experience a complete personality change
when a substitute teacher walks into the classroom.
Who knew? Any teacher who has ever had a substitute!

As a new teacher, I made many mistakes, mostly due to lack of experience. One of the biggest mistakes I made was not realizing that my students, in my absence, would take advantage of a substitute teacher. I'll never forget the following event.

It was my first year of teaching, and I had to attend a meeting. It was going to be the first day of school that I had ever missed. Still wearing my rose-colored glasses and never having left my seventh graders in the hands of a substitute teacher, I never anticipated what "could" and probably "would" happen during my absence. I thought I had all of my bases covered. I had left explicit instructions for the substitute teacher – down to the last detail. I told my students I would be out, that a substitute teacher would be with them, and that I would see them the day after. By this time, I had my classroom management system well organized. My students knew what I expected, and they followed all of my procedures beautifully. So I had nothing to worry about. Right? Oh, how very wrong! I returned the following day to learn that my little "angels" had turned into raging devils in the hands of the substitute. The substitute vowed never to come near my class again. She was devastated, and so was I. How could this have happened? What had gone wrong? I learned the hard way that I had missed one crucial step. Yes, I had provided the substitute teacher with explicit instructions, but I had completely forgotten about the instructions for my students. So just as the poor, unsuspecting substitute teacher vowed never to enter my classroom doors again, I vowed never to let such a situation occur again should I be absent. The solution was quite simple, and it worked like a charm! The next time I had a meeting to attend, this is what I did, step by step:

♦ I told my students I would be absent and that I would need them to take over the classroom and help the substitute teacher. I made a big deal over that fact that I knew I could trust them, so I was not at all worried about whether or not things would run smoothly.

◆ I assigned roles to each student. For instance, one student had the task of welcoming the substitute and showing her where everything was located on my desk. Another student had the job of handing out the bell-work assignment to students as they entered the classroom. Another student had the job of giving the signal for quiet when the substitute was ready to begin and sharing that same signal with the substitute so that she could use it also. Another student had the job of explaining all of the daily procedures to the substitute. Another had the job of picking up assignments from students as they finished their work. I kept creating "jobs" until every student had one. One student even had the job of presenting the substitute teacher with a small gift at the end of the class period. Another had the job of "beginning the applause" after the gift was given. All students shared the job of thanking the substitute on their way out of the classroom, and one student was assigned to remind any student who forgot. Okay, you get the picture.

◆ On the day before I was to be absent, we practiced by pretending that I was the substitute. The students loved the idea, because now they were in charge of running the classroom and helping to make things easy on the substitute teacher. They had specific responsibilities, and they took pride in that fact.

◆ I wrote down all the responsibilities of every student, and each received a copy. This would help to ensure that they would hold each other accountable or simply remind each other if one of them forgot his or her assigned job.

◆ We also discussed the fact that this same plan would remain in place if I were ever absent due to illness. For this, we kept extra "gifts" in the closet.

Results? I returned the day after my absence to find a two-page letter from the substitute. She said to PLEASE call her if I ever needed a substitute again. She went on to say that she had never witnessed anything like it. For each class period, she was amazed at how helpful and cooperative the students were. "And can you believe that they actually clapped for me at the end of the class? I've never received applause in my life! And I believe that every single one of them stopped to thank me on the way out." You see, the students had played their roles so well that she didn't even realize that most of it had been rehearsed and that they were *supposed* to stop and thank her on their way out. But even if she did realize it was staged and practiced, she appreciated it nonetheless.

The students couldn't wait to brag about how well they had run the class without me! It worked for me every time I used it over the years. The technique is used successfully at all grade levels. I've even used it with a college class just to prove that the technique works for all ages. It will work for you, too! Put your own spin on it, but remember to have a job for everyone in the event of your absence.

> ✔**Ask Yourself:** Do I have a plan to ensure that if I am absent, my students can assist the substitute teacher to make sure that the classroom runs like a well-oiled machine? Do each of the students have assigned roles, and have we practiced the plan ahead of time?

Planning: Section Highlights

◆ Set aside a specific time each day for planning and grading – away from distractions. Remember that you can get a lot more done in an hour of uninterrupted time than you can in several hours of interrupted time.

◆ Remind yourself, often, that the rewards of touching young lives far outweigh the demands and challenges of teaching.

◆ Avoid procrastination at all costs. Stay on top of your workload.

◆ Plan lessons with clear objectives and activities designed to maximize student interest and engagement.

◆ Remain organized and prepared in order to provide a safe, clutter-free, welcoming space for your students to learn and thrive.

◆ Maintain accurate records in order to track student progress, to identify patterns in student learning and behavior, to adjust teaching accordingly, and to communicate effectively with parents.

◆ Ensure that, for every lesson, your students know what they are learning and why they are learning it.

◆ Provide (and practice) a specific "substitute teacher day" plan so that students are prepared to assist, not resist, a substitute teacher.

◆ Remember that being over-prepared is never a problem in the classroom. Being under-prepared is ALWAYS a problem.

Section Three

Instruction

Make It Real

I just don't see the point in why I need to know this junk
You say if I don't learn it, then surely I will flunk
But I need a better reason for learning all this stuff
It's boring and it's pointless, so learning it is rough
And every time I'm bored in school, I think of other things
Lost inside a daydream until the school bell rings
Which means I haven't learned it, which means my grades are bad
Which means that I'm in trouble and my mom and dad are mad
And then I get so far behind that it's just too late to pass
So next year here I am again – I'm right back in your class
I didn't get it last year; I don't get it today
Please, teacher, make it real for me so that I can move on in May!

Tip 31
Learn to Recover Quickly

Our greatest glory is not in never falling, but in rising every time we fall.
—Confucius

One of the biggest mistakes that new teachers make is being afraid to ask for help or admit to mistakes for fear of appearing *stupid*. Well, here are a few facts:

◆ New teachers are not supposed to know it all. They make mistakes.

◆ Veteran teachers are not supposed to know it all. They make mistakes.

◆ No one knows it all. Everyone makes mistakes.

◆ Anyone who acts like a "know-it-all" is attempting to hide the fact that he doesn't know much of anything! And anyone who is not making mistakes is not doing much of anything!

Teachers, even the best of them, make mistakes. We are, after all, human. And know that you will continue to make mistakes because no one has ever "finished" learning to teach. One of the differences between effective teachers and ineffective teachers is that effective teachers know how to recover from their mistakes quickly. When they make a mistake, they readily admit it. If at all possible, they correct it. And then they move on. Ineffective teachers try to hide behind defensiveness, thus making the mistake a bigger deal than it usually is and preventing themselves from earning the respect of their students. If students see that you never admit to your mistakes, then they will be reluctant to admit to theirs. Without meaning to, by not ever admitting to a mistake, you inadvertently model that mistakes are just not okay. And isn't that the direct opposite of what we want to teach our students? So shouldn't we model what we want them to emulate?

When you say something you should not have said, when you inadvertently hurt a student's feelings, when you give incorrect information, etc., apologize immediately and correct the mistake if possible. Acknowledge your mistake and then let it go. By doing this, you will earn the respect of those you work with and those you teach, and you will be teaching others that mistakes, if handled appropriately, can provide wonderful opportunities for learning and growing. As the old song goes, "Pick yourself up, dust yourself off, and start all over again."

✔ **Ask Yourself:** When I make a mistake, do I serve as a good role model for students by admitting it, recovering quickly, and learning from it?

Tip 32
Teach Students at Their Level

QUESTIONS: At whose level did you learn to speak? To walk?
To swim? To ride a bike? At your level or at the neighbor's kid's level?

I have always been baffled by the age-old questions asked time and again by educators: "At what level should we teach students? Should we teach them at their own level or at grade level?" Think about this: When you first learned to speak, you learned at YOUR level. It didn't matter that other babies of your age spoke sooner or later than you did. You had to be ready. You couldn't have possibly learned to speak at anyone else's level. So you learned at your level, and today you can speak. When you learned to walk, it was at YOUR level. It didn't matter that some babies walked as early as seven months and you did not walk until 13 months. No one panicked. They simply waited until you were ready. You learned at your level, and today you can walk. And so it went for any skill you learned as you were growing up – that is, until you went to school. Then you were possibly expected to read before you were ready, which, of course, is impossible – but hey, lots of other kids your age could do it. And if you were forced to attempt skills at levels above your own, then you experienced failure, which, of course, bred more failure. **The simple fact is that none of us can learn anything at anyone else's level**. However, if we are taken from our level and moved forward, one step at a time, then there's no stopping us!

I have had the privilege of knowing, for many years, a teacher who understands that students must be taught at their own levels. She teaches in a middle school where the population is impoverished and most of the students are considered *at risk*. Her students consist of *alternative* students – seventh graders who have been retained as many as three times, many of whom are 15 years old. Her task is to teach, in one school year, both the seventh- and eighth-grade curriculums to these students in order to prepare them for the eighth grade statewide criterion-referenced test. If they pass the test, they move on to the ninth grade. Now remember that these students are considerably behind *typical* seventh graders in their achievement. The task seems insurmountable, and most teachers would say it's impossible. Are you ready for the results? This teacher's students have almost a 90% passing rate on the statewide test. In fact, their passing rate is above both the district and the state levels! How does this teacher do it? How does she take students who have trouble writing complete sentences and get them to write structured essays in under eight months? In her words: "I teach them at their own levels. If they can't write a sentence, even though they're *supposed* to be able to write sentences at their age, I simply teach them how to write a sentence. When they're ready, we move on to writing paragraphs and then eventually essays. I make sure that they experience nothing but success, and it becomes a habit – a way of thinking."

I guess it is true that "common sense is not necessarily common." If all teachers took all students from where they were and moved them forward to where they could be (as opposed to teaching them at the level they're "supposed" to be), the student achievement in our nation's schools would skyrocket! Now let's be realistic and admit that meeting individual learner needs is not easy. It's an outright juggling act. But consider the alternative. . . .

Remember, we teach STUDENTS. And the only way to teach students is AT THEIR LEVELS!

> Teach me at my level, for that is where I revel
> My behavior, then, might be more of an angel than a devil
> And once success is mine, there will be no stopping me
> So teach me at my level and achievement's what you'll see!

✔**Ask Yourself:** Do I tend to teach all students as if they are at one level, or do I realize that students are at different levels and can only succeed when I meet them there?

Tip 33
Observe Other Teachers

By watching other teachers in action,
Without having my own class as a distraction
I can see what works and what does not.
By observing others, I can learn a lot!

When I graduated from college, I went straight into my own classroom. That classroom is where I lived, basically. I met my co-workers, but I never had the privilege of seeing them teach. I did ask lots of questions, and they were always happy to share their secrets and their wisdom. However, I never got to see them in action. Then, one day, my eyes were opened. I was placed on a committee whose job it was to observe all of the teachers in a neighboring school currently implementing a particular program. For the first time since I began teaching, I got to observe other teachers teaching. It was wonderful! I learned so much in that one day. In the effective teachers' classrooms, I learned better ways of dealing with students – behaviorally and academically. In less effective teachers' classrooms, I learned a lot about what not to do. But in all of the classrooms, I LEARNED and I instantly became a better teacher!

Teaching continues to be a very "isolated" profession. We spend the majority of our time in our own classrooms and rarely see beyond our four walls! Yet **collaboration has proven time and again to be very beneficial, rejuvenating, and enlightening for teachers.** So why don't we do more of it? Some of our best ideas are "stolen" from other teachers. And the good news is that teachers are generous people, always happy to share their successes with others. Go into an online teacher chat, ask a question, and prepare to be astounded with wonderful ideas you'll receive from teachers worldwide! But ask teachers how many opportunities they have had to observe other teachers teaching and many will tell you that these opportunities have been rare. If you are a mentor, don't just observe the teacher you are mentoring. Allow that teacher to learn from observing you and others. Just as it's crucial that we model the skills we teach our students, so must mentors model good teaching for the teachers they're mentoring. **If you are a new teacher, ask your administrator to schedule some time for you to observe your mentor and others.** If finding time is a problem, ask your mentor to video a short segment of him- or herself teaching and send an electronic copy of the video to you. Then you can watch at your convenience. There is so much to be learned from watching others. Oh, and don't sell yourself short. Your mentor will also be learning from watching you!

> ✔**Ask Yourself:** Do I have the opportunity to observe my mentor and others in their classrooms? If not, what can I do to make that happen?

Tip 34
Refrain from Lecturing

Teach, teach, teach away
Preach, preach all the day
You'd save your voice and I'd learn more, too
If you'd stop talking and let me <u>do</u>!

Parent: What did you learn in school today?
Child: I learned swimming.
Parent: They taught you to swim?
Child: No, they taught me swimming.
Parent: So you can swim now?
Child: No, but I know swimming. Ask me any question you want about swimming.
Parent: The only important question is, "Can you swim?"
Child: I don't know. I haven't tried yet.

FACT: Lecturing is the one of the LEAST effective means of instructing, yet it is still widely used! To make that point clear, let's imagine that you are learning a new skill – you are learning to swim. Your instructor seats you and 20 other novices in desks beside the pool. He lectures to you on swimming and you take notes. You literally hear everything there is to know about swimming because your instructor is an advanced swimmer. He knows his stuff! All of his information is accurate, so you are receiving "good" instruction. In fact, he even gets into the pool and models good swimming for you. After memorizing everything there is to know about swimming, you take the exam: a written test. You have put much time and effort into your studies, and you ace the exam. You are now a good swimmer. Right? Wrong! We don't learn to swim by listening to great lectures on swimming. We learn to swim by swimming. We don't learn to drive a car by listening to informative lectures on driving. We learn by actually "doing" the driving. So it is in life, and so it is in the classroom. This is not to say that there is never a place for lecturing, but lecturing does not teach us to *do* anything. Great writers did not become great writers because they listened to lectures and memorized all of the *rules*. Good readers did not become good readers by listening to lectures on reading. They became adept at their skills through *doing*. Great historians did not become great historians by listening to lectures and memorizing history. They actually dove in and swam around in history. I've often heard it said, "The one who does the doing does the learning." I have yet to hear it said that the one who can listen really intently to great lectures does the learning. Perhaps I missed that particular lecture!

> ✔ **Ask Yourself:** Who does most of the "doing" in my classroom? Am I often engaging my students in activities that foster "listening" or actual "doing"?

Tip 35
Refrain from "Textbook Teaching"

I know of no adults who owe their successes to the efficacy of a textbook, but of many who owe their successes to the influence of a teacher.

—Annette Breaux

No, I am not suggesting that you throw away your trusty textbooks. I can think of very few teachers who do not use textbooks. Textbooks, in paper or digital format, are valuable resources. But that is the key – they are *resources*. I witnessed a conversation in a faculty lounge that went like this: "Can you believe that they've adopted this new textbook? I can't teach from that. I'm going to continue to use the textbook I've been using. I'm not about to change all of my lesson plans because of a new textbook. Also, this textbook has too much material to cover in one school year. I can cover the textbook I'm using now in exactly one school year." This brought to mind another teacher who used to have his students, on the first day of school, actually *sit* on their textbooks. He would then say, "Okay, we have now *covered* the textbook." This is not to say that he did not use the textbook. He did. But he used it as a supplement to his teaching. The textbook did not make his instructional decisions. He made his instructional decisions based on the needs of his students. So should we all. Most districts have very specific curriculums, and no textbook has an exact correlation to any district's curriculum. However, when selecting textbooks, districts consider those that have the closest correlation to their curriculums. Often, however, teachers see the textbook as the definitive curriculum. They cover the book from beginning to end, neglecting to teach much of the district's curriculum. **The effective teacher begins with the curriculum and then determines the best resources available to teach that curriculum.** The ineffective teacher depends on textbooks to tell him what to teach, when to teach it, what questions to ask, what answers the students should give, and to provide him with formatted tests and answer keys to everything he has *covered*. Remember: textbooks are resources. We teach students, not textbooks.

> ✔**Ask Yourself:** If all of the textbooks were removed from my classroom, would I be able to continue my teaching? If your answer is *no*, then you are relying too heavily on the textbook in your instruction.

Tip 36
Teach Social Skills

If people had better social skills, there would be fewer social ills.

Assume nothing! Don't expect students to come to you with good manners, to know right from wrong, to work cooperatively with others. Some will, but many won't. I often hear it said that parents should be responsible for teaching social skills. I'm not arguing that point. But the fact remains that **many students learn good social skills from their parents and many do not.** So where do we find time to *fit it into* the overloaded curriculum? We begin by being good models. And then we weave social skills into everything we teach. I knew a teacher who complained about her students having no manners or social skills. When I asked how she incorporated social skills into her teaching, she said, "I don't. It's not my job." Upon observing her, I noticed that not only did she refrain from teaching social skills, but she also refrained from modeling them. She was loud, she displayed negative body language, she never said *please* or *thank you*, and her lessons were boring. Students worked alone, and it's tough to learn social skills without the benefit of social interaction! Out of curiosity, I observed the same students with another teacher. Not surprisingly, they were no longer ill-behaved. This teacher greeted her students with a smile; she thanked them often; she took time, when introducing a group activity, to discuss proper behavior; and she basically did the exact opposite of the first teacher. Thus, she got opposite behavior!

I went back to the first teacher and said, "I agree that your students are a little lacking in social skills." "A little lacking?" she asked. "Try ground zero!" "Okay," I said. "I'm going to help you to turn that around, if you're willing." "Sure," she said. "I'll try anything." Without telling her what I had observed in the other teacher's classroom, I simply gave her a list of what the other teacher was doing. I had her do five things: 1) greet students every day as if you are happy to see them, 2) speak with a pleasant tone, and don't lose your temper at any cost, 3) thank your students for appropriate behavior, 4) explain what proper behavior looks like well in advance of activities, and 5) allow more student interaction.

I observed her for five days. Following each observation, I provided feedback, and we discussed changes in student behavior. By the end of the week, she was a new person, and her students were different students. To this

Section 3. Tip 36

day, she thanks me for helping her to change. She has never said, "Thanks for helping my students to behave." Instead, she realizes that SHE made the difference. Remember that *students emulate what you do, so the things you 'model' will stick like glue!*

> ✔ **Ask Yourself:** Do I model the same behaviors I'd like to foster in my students?

Tip 37
Focus on Students' Strengths

Point out all my weaknesses, and those are all you'll see,
But focus on my strengths instead, and stronger I will be.

Quick activity: Think of two of your most challenging students. Get them clearly in your mind. Now list 10 strengths and 10 weaknesses of each. Was it easier to come up with the weaknesses? If so, you are not alone. Most teachers are far more adept at spotting student weaknesses than they are at identifying student strengths. But since success truly does breed success, **we need to turn our thinking around and begin focusing on the strengths of each student.** A teacher once insisted to me that she had three students who made her entire life miserable. I asked her to tell me about the strengths of each, and she answered, "None of them have any strengths." No wonder these students were causing problems in the classroom. They were considered "hopeless" in the eyes of their teacher. **Every student possesses lots of strengths.** At times we have to search a little harder and dig a little deeper to find them, but they're there.

I observed these three students – all of whom happened to be boys – in this teacher's classroom, and then I followed the three boys into another teacher's classroom. Seeing that these students experienced *personality* changes in the second teacher's classroom, I decided to speak to the second teacher. I asked her to tell me about each boy, listing his strengths and weaknesses. Her comments were: "Wendell is very polite. He does struggle with the content, but he gives 100% in effort. He has wonderful leadership abilities, and he has a heart of gold. His handwriting is meticulous, and his work is always done so neatly. He's also a very good listener." The comments about the other two boys were very similar in that they focused on strengths as opposed to weaknesses. I then asked the teacher what she did differently with Wendell, since he had trouble grasping the content. She answered, "I provide remediation activities, and then he catches on because he's so willing and determined. I also give him lots of responsibilities around the classroom because he handles responsibility very well. I just do things that help to ensure his success every day, and the growth in him has been phenomenal!" Wow! What a difference. Same students. Different teachers. You decide.

> ✔ **Ask Yourself:** Can I list several strengths of each of my students? If not, find those strengths quickly and begin to focus on them. You'll be astonished by the positive results!

Tip 38
Allow and Encourage Students to Work Together

As the world becomes more complicated, so we are less and less able to carry through anything to a successful conclusion without the collaboration of others.
—Alexander Fleming

It is often stated that any teacher who argues against encouraging students to work cooperatively has never encouraged students to work cooperatively. Life is about cooperation. How well you do or don't learn to cooperate with others will eventually determine how well you will or won't succeed. But don't expect students to come to you possessing all of the skills they need in order to work cooperatively with others. That's why they need us. We're here to teach them.

Much research has been conducted on the power of cooperative learning. The results have been consistent: **Students who engage in cooperative learning activities develop problem-solving skills, develop better social skills, and achieve at higher levels.** So why is it that so many teachers, of all grade levels, tend to avoid the idea of having students work together in cooperative learning environments? Once again, we must look back at classroom management. The following are actual teachers' answers to the question, "Why don't you use cooperative learning activities in your classroom?"

- ◆ I've tried letting my students work together, but they can't get along with one another.
- ◆ I put my students in groups, and one person does all of the work.
- ◆ I don't want to hold back the stronger students because of the weaker ones.
- ◆ Cooperative learning equals chaos. I want structure and order in my classroom.
- ◆ Today's students simply cannot work together.
- ◆ I tried cooperative learning once, and my students argued with one another.
- ◆ I like a quiet classroom. I'm not about to put my students in groups where all they'll do is talk.

Notice that in all of the aforementioned answers, the issues of order, structure, noise, lack of on-task behavior, and chaos are evident. Again, **all point to problems in classroom management**. Yes, the aforementioned fears can become realities, but NOT with true cooperative learning conducted in a well-managed environment. The key here is structure. It is impossible to do justice to describing cooperative learning completely here. But, in a nutshell, this is what true cooperative learning looks like:

- Students are assigned to groups consisting of various personality types, interests, ability levels, and so on. These groups are not fixed. They may change often. This allows you to differentiate instruction to meet everyone's unique needs.
- Each student in the group has a specific job in carrying out the overall charge of the group.
- All activities are highly structured.
- Appropriate behaviors in the group are taught, modeled, and practiced.
- Noise levels are under control, and all "noise" is "structured" noise.
- Students of all ability levels are challenged to think critically and to solve problems cooperatively, just like in the real world.
- Procedures for each aspect of group interaction are clearly established from day one.
- Students are involved in the group's mission, and they experience high levels of success.

Sometimes working cooperatively happens in pairs. The teacher pairs students and allows them to work together in solving a problem, finding an answer to a question, creating something, working on a project, or discussing an issue. During class discussions, students often find it less intimidating to answer questions in pairs than they do alone. But this, too, is highly structured.

If you haven't yet attempted to allow your students to work together, reach out to a mentor, a colleague, or fellow educators on social media sites who are already doing this successfully. You'll get more ideas than you can possibly implement. Just pick one strategy or idea that appeals to you and start from there. Then slowly build on that until you have your students cooperating and collaborating effortlessly and successfully. Remember, however, that before implementing any type of cooperative group activities, effective classroom management must be in place.

✔**Ask Yourself:** Do my students know how to work together – to cooperate with one another? And do I provide the opportunities and structure they need in order to work together successfully?

Tip 39
Relate Lessons to Real Life

Why Do We Have to Know This?

"Why do we have to know this?" asked the student, looking confused.
His classmates echoed his sentiments and their teacher was not amused,
But the fact remains that people learn best when they know what they're learning
  and WHY,
So connect what you teach to your students' real lives, and watch them succeed
  and comply!

If you are a new teacher, just starting out, with a long, successful career of teaching ahead of you, then I will go out on a limb here and assume you're not interested in attending the meeting this afternoon for soon-to-be teacher retirees. If your savings account is a little at the shallow end of the pool, I'll assume you're not currently researching where to invest hundreds of thousands of dollars. Right? These topics are of no interest to you because you simply cannot relate to them.

Aristotle said, "All knowledge is relational." In other words, in order for us to learn anything new, we must have something we already "know" with which to connect the new skill. When work makes sense to us, we have a purpose for doing it. If it does not seem meaningful, we close our minds to it. After all, **what's the point in learning something that has no meaning in our lives?** I often hear students say that they *hate* English or they *hate* reading. However, I have yet to encounter students who *hate* English or reading when it comes to texting or posting on social media sites or reading the menu at their favorite fast-food restaurant, or when they want to browse through the television listings.

Let's drive this point home with a classroom experience that most, if not all, of us have had. We all learned about *nouns* in a similar fashion. In fact, our experiences were so similar, no matter where we went to school, that it's almost frightening. It went like this:

The teacher began the lesson by saying, "Open your English books to page 27." We all sighed, as though we were being tortured. At the top of the page it said, "Nouns." We had to copy that title into our notebooks. Then we had to copy the definition that said, "A noun names a person, place, or thing." Then we

categorized people, places, and things. Next we did Exercise A where we had
to underline the nouns. Following Exercise A, we did Exercise B. We did the
worksheet on nouns after that.

What did any of this have to do with our actual lives other than the fact that we
may have wanted to pass the test, which was, of course, on Friday? That, by the
way, is NOT a real-life connection! Is it any wonder that even English-speaking
students claim to hate English or any other subject that is taught in this fashion?

Now let's consider a completely different scenario. Notice that it takes
no extra time or work. It simply involves asking yourself the question that
all great teachers ask themselves when planning any lesson: "How does this
particular skill or content affect the lives of my students today?"

The teacher begins the lesson by saying, "You don't need to take a thing out
right now. Maya, tell me about something you did yesterday, but do not name
any people, any places, or any things." Maya says, "My brother and . . . " And
the teacher interrupts and says, "Oops, your brother is a person." Then she says,
"went to the mall . . ." and the teacher interrupts and says, "No, the mall is a
place." And Maya is having difficulty. The teacher then asks another student
to help by telling something he did yesterday, without, of course, naming any
people, places, or things. Within seconds, the students figure out that the task
is impossible. The teacher says, "Oh, so you're telling me that without people,
places, and things, you cannot speak in a way that makes sense? Okay, then
write a sentence (or a pretend text message on paper) about something you did
yesterday without naming any people, places, or things." As the students get
busy, the teacher walks around and has each student cross out any word that is
a person, place, or thing. When everyone has finished, they begin to share their
sentences. Tim reads his. It sounds like this: "A it the at the in the." The students
laugh and realize that writing makes no sense either without including people,
places, or things. The teacher then says, "So you're telling me that you could not
speak or write or even THINK without people, places, and things? They're called
nouns, by the way. Okay, so how would your life be different if nothing you said
made sense to anyone anymore?" A discussion follows as to the relevance of
nouns in all of our lives.

**Do you see how the teacher has gotten the students to understand the
real-life connection and its importance in their lives? That's teaching!**
Afterwards, if the teacher chooses to use the textbook definition and to have
the students complete exercises A and B, that is fine, as the relevance of what

they're doing has been established! I'll bet that some of you reading this are thinking to yourselves, "I've never even thought about nouns that way!" That's because it was never taught to you in that way, so you never stopped to analyze the importance of every facet of the language.

How can we, as teachers, expect our students to *buy into* something for which they see no meaning? We can't! So make that real-life connection with every skill you teach. And if you ever come across a skill that truly has no real-life connection, then we should remove that skill from the curriculum. Oh, and the infamous question, "Why do we have to know this?" is a red flag to you that you have not made that critical *real-life* connection! Making it REAL has tremendous APPEAL!

> ✔**Ask Yourself:** When planning a lesson, do I first ask myself why students need this particular knowledge or skill in their current lives and then plan accordingly?

Tip 40
Use Classroom Technology Effectively

If we teach today as we taught yesterday, we rob our children of tomorrow.
—John Dewey

Technology is, indisputably, a main artery to the heart of today's world. It is woven into almost every aspect of our lives. So it's no longer an option for teachers to say, "I'm just no good with technology." That's akin to saying, "I'm just no good at teaching today's students," because today's students are surrounded by technology, far beyond their video games and smart phones. If we're going to teach today's learners and prepare them for today's (and tomorrow's) world, we have to continually learn to use technology appropriately and integrate it effectively into our lessons.

The following is a list of only a few ways in which effective teachers incorporate technology into their classrooms:

- Set up a class web page to share what's going on in the classroom, to communicate with parents, to post information on upcoming assignments, projects, etc. The possibilities are endless.
- Create digital flashcards.
- Send students on virtual scavenger hunts.
- Communicate with other students in classrooms almost anywhere in the world through videoconferencing.
- Use online graph makers, map makers, rubric creators, mind map creators, etc.
- Use free online software that allows students to write stories, adding digital illustrations, videos, narration, etc.
- Access free online learning games available in all subject areas.
- Have students participate in online goal setting and progress tracking.
- Use virtual manipulatives to teach math concepts.
- Use online, interactive, leveled books to provide practice for students at various reading levels.

- Create games in any subject (using online software) for the purpose of review, remediation, or meaningful practice for early finishers.
- Allow students to do online projects, create slide presentations, conduct internet research, etc.
- Use digital encyclopedias, thesauruses, and dictionaries.
- Access free online game shows designed for student learning in all subject areas.
- Conduct online surveys.
- Have students create digital books.
- Create digital, interactive posters, maps, and more.
- Set up a digital photo frame with pictures of your students involved in learning tasks. These photos can be updated as often as you like.
- Create digital comic strips.
- Access free online lesson plans and activities in any subject area.
- Use free online class polling.
- Allow students to blog and create podcasts.
- Use interactive whiteboards.
- Show students how to take digital notes.
- Tour virtual museums.
- Go on virtual field trips to anywhere on Earth and into outer space!

✔ **Ask Yourself:** Do I maximize the use of available technology to enhance teaching and learning?

Tip from Breaux, A. and Whitaker, T. (2015). *Seven Simple Secrets: What the BEST Teachers Know and Do! 2nd edition.* New York: Routledge.

Tip 41
Avoid Homework Overload

Moderation in all things, especially homework!
—ALL students

Parents complain about homework, students complain about homework, and teachers complain about how their students do not turn in homework. **No one seems to be too crazy about the idea of homework, yet some teachers keep piling it on.** Imagine if a student has six teachers and each assigns homework activities that require 20 minutes of work. That's two hours, IF the student understands the concepts and does not struggle. Where does he find time to be a kid? Also, many students are involved in after-school activities. Is it any wonder that parents get upset about excessive homework assignments and many students do not even complete their homework assignments?

As the saying goes, "Everything in moderation." Students spend between seven and eight hours a day at school. Does it make sense to send them home with hours of work? If I, the teacher, work hard every day with my students, then homework should not be a nightly event.

Much controversy surrounds the topic of *homework*. Do students need homework? Does it improve achievement? Does it foster responsibility? Should it affect student grades? To date, the jury is still out on the homework issue. You can find plenty of research to support it. You can find plenty of research to contradict that research. You can find teachers who believe it is vital. You can find teachers who believe it is a waste of time. Most teachers fall somewhere in the middle.

I am not opposed to homework, but here are my suggestions:

1. Assign homework in moderation.
2. Make any homework assignments interesting, meaningful, and doable.
3. Remember that the old trick of doubling the homework if they don't do it has never worked. (If they didn't do it once, they won't do it twice!)
4. Remember that many students do not have the luxury of parental help with homework.
5. Be very careful about allowing a missed homework assignment to affect a student's grade. Aren't grades supposed to represent what a student

Imagine teaching someone to ride a bike without ever showing them what bike riding *looks like*. That would be ludicrous, yet we do it every day in the classroom! Teaching, in any form, requires modeling.

> ✔ **Ask Yourself:** For every lesson you plan, ask yourself a very important question: How do I plan to model this new skill for my students so that they can "see" what they will eventually be able to do?

Tip 43
Make Learning Fun

Don't look so serious when you're teaching, please don't!
If you don't have fun, then the students won't,
So take every lesson and teach it with zest
And you'll get from your students their very best!

While I was conducting a presentation on effective teaching strategies for high school and university teachers, a college professor volunteered the following: "When I walked into the training today and learned of the activities that were going to be conducted, I almost walked out. I thought it was going to be 'elementary.' However, after participating in the activities and having fun doing so, I realized that if I could have fun, maybe my students could have fun as opposed to just listening to my daily lectures. And maybe I'd even have fun teaching!" In response, a high school teacher enthusiastically added, "I do 'elementary' activities with my students every day, and they love it!" When I asked what she meant by "elementary" activities, she explained that she uses lots of cooperative learning, learning games, hands-on activities, group discussion, and very little lecture. "My students love to come to class, because they have fun and they experience so much success." A very interesting discussion ensued where we discussed the fact that students learn best when they are having fun. "Adults do too!" added one of the participants.

Too often I encounter teachers who think that teaching and learning should be "serious business." Their demeanors are serious, their classrooms are serious places, their students are bored out of their minds, and discipline problems are evident. That's not very conducive to inspiring students to achieve! **The truth is that we all learn best when the learning environment is interesting, exciting, and inviting.** Some teachers are afraid to allow their students to have "fun" in their classrooms for fear of losing control of discipline. This is a mistake, in that **"fun" and "chaos" are not synonymous.** Chaos is a classroom management problem. If classroom management is well established, there will be no chaos. The best teachers know that in the most effective learning environments classroom management is established, students are actively involved in the learning, lessons and activities are highly structured, meaningful, and interesting, and students are enjoying the learning process. Yes, they are having fun! Remember that taking teaching seriously and treating teaching as a strictly serious business are two very different things. **If there's not a big kid living inside of you, there's not a great teacher coming out of you!** So channel your inner child and lighten up, add excitement to your lessons, and watch your students' achievement increase. Your students will enjoy their learning, you will enjoy your teaching, and you will all have fun.

✔**Ask Yourself:** Are my students having fun in my classroom every day? Would my students describe me an enthusiastic and fun-loving teacher? If not, what do I need to do in order to change that?

Tip 44
Encourage Active Student Participation

I hear and I forget.
I see and I remember.
I do and I understand.

—Chinese Proverb

Imagine that you are a student in a classroom where every day is the same. You walk into class, you open your textbook, the teacher lectures, and you take notes. You read a chapter, answer the questions at the end of the chapter, and complete worksheets. You define 20 vocabulary words, all of which must be memorized (along with your notes) for Friday's test. The teacher does the talking, and you do the sitting. You are expected to pay attention, be interested, keep quiet, and master your lessons. Imagine going through this every day for an entire school year! Where is the *teaching* in what I have just described? How much "sitting still" can any student endure? Where's the "doing" on the part of the students? Where are students actually solving problems or thinking critically? When has this type of teaching ever increased ANY student's achievement?

Now consider that you are a student in a classroom where no two days are alike. You have been studying the Civil War. The class has conducted research followed by discussions where students have interacted with the research and voiced opinions. Today, you are assigned to groups. Each group will be writing its thoughts on the war from different viewpoints: a Confederate soldier, a Union soldier, a slave owner, a slave, and the mother of a soldier. In completing your assignment, you will be conducting online research. The teacher will interact with each group. Then, each group will present its perspective and findings to the class. Discussions will follow each presentation. Can you see the difference between this lesson and the previous one? Did you recognize the teaching here, the active student participation, the interest level, the meaningful learning, and the lack of boredom? In which class would you prefer to be a student???

To rephrase the Chinese proverb on the previous page, "What I hear in the classroom goes in one ear and out the other, what I see in the classroom I tend to remember seeing, but what I actually have to do, I learn, and the learning sticks because I understand."

> ✔ **Ask Yourself:** Are my students actively DOING or passively ENDURING?

Tip 45
Challenge Students to Think Critically

I may be smarter than you or I know
So challenge me to think, and we'll both know if that's so!

A young boy I met at a friend's house enthusiastically told me that his favorite subject was math. He went on to tell me that he knew all of his multiplication facts very well. I obliged him by quizzing him. Sure enough, he knew the answers. When I asked him what was 4 × 4, he readily answered, "16." Then I asked, "What does that mean?" Again, he answered "16." I realized that the student had no concept of what multiplication actually meant. So the teacher in me broke into a quick lesson. After I explained the concept behind multiplication, he said, "Oh! Is that what that means? Do you mean that if I have four groups of people with four people in each group, that's the same as saying 4 + 4 + 4 + 4 or 4 × 4 = 16? I never knew that!" He immediately grabbed a deck of cards and started arranging them into groups and coming up with his own multiplication facts, delighted with the fact that multiplication was really addition in groups. I then had to sit with him and share in his enthusiasm, ignoring the group of adults with whom I had previously been visiting. The light bulb had gone on in a child's mind, and there was no turning it off. Beautiful!

The point I'm trying to make is that **we, as teachers, often assume too much. Just because a student knows an answer or can memorize a given piece of information, we assume that he understands.** This is often not the case. Knowing informational facts and being able to apply that information by thinking critically and using the information to solve problems are two different things.

Critical thinking involves problem solving, which fosters a true understanding of a concept. Think about this. How many times, in your adult life, have you had to regurgitate the important battles of World War II? You *learned* them in your schooling, but unless you are a history buff, you probably don't remember them, nor do you need to in order to get along in life. What was important was to understand the reasons behind World War II: how and why it began, how and why we, as a nation, became involved, how people's lives were affected because of it, and how life as we know it today is influenced by the history that preceded it.

As a *fun* experiment, I took a group of 32 ninth graders and asked them to identify pronouns in a given set of sentences. With three exceptions, they were all able to complete the task successfully and accurately. Then I asked, "Now why do we have pronouns in our language, and how would life be different without them?" I received blank stares. Nothing. No answers. Then I had all of them attempt to tell me something about themselves without using pronouns. (You may want to attempt it yourself before you read on.) Within a minute, the students suddenly saw how awkward and cumbersome the language would be without the use of pronouns. It made sense! Then I took the three students who had had a little trouble with pronouns, provided quick remediation, and the light went on for them, too!

We need to make a special effort in our teaching to stop doling out facts and start encouraging students to think critically. Once they understand a concept, the facts become meaningful. This is the kind of thinking that arouses students' interest, encourages them to delve deeply into concepts, and urges them to remain in a continual state of questioning.

✔**Ask Yourself:** Do I often have my students explain, compare, devise, determine, analyze, evaluate, and just plain old "figure out" why or how when they are learning?

Tip 46
Use Authentic Means of Assessment

How much sense would it make for a person to take a written
exam on riding a bicycle in order to determine whether
he can actually ride a bicycle???

There is much debate in education and lots of controversy over the best means of assessing student work. Without any research and without any controversy, I will put the whole idea of authentic assessment into perspective for you. The word *authentic* means *real* or *valid*. **So, authentic assessment is a valid way of measuring whether your students have attained a particular skill.** In the question above, even the slightest bit of common sense reveals that assessing the skill of riding a bicycle with a written test is ludicrous. Authentic assessment of this skill would require that the student actually ride the bicycle. So it is with any skill that we teach. In order to determine a student's knowledge of particular vocabulary, regurgitating a memorized definition tells us nothing. The student must actually be able to *use* the vocabulary words. **A written test on a scientific method is not valid if the student is only required to list the steps in the scientific method. He must be able to apply the method to a given experiment.** Giving a set of questions based on a story that has been discussed all week in class is really a test in memory as opposed to a test in reading comprehension. In order to know if students can truly comprehend what they read, they must be tested with unfamiliar text.

If you want to know if a person can cook, then have the person cook something. Apply that same logic in your classroom. If you are teaching your students how to design web pages, then assess them, following thorough instruction, by actually having them design a web page. Although a written quiz on designing a web page may provide insight into whether they understand the steps they will have to follow in designing a web page, it's not enough because they will still need to show you if they can apply those steps to the actual task. In assessing student work, decide what skill you want to assess, and then assess it in a way that is "real" and "valid." It's really that simple!

> ✔ **Ask Yourself:** Do I decide, in the planning stage, what skills I will be assessing and then teach and assess those skills in a way that shows whether students actually possess those skills? If so, you've got it!

Tip 47
Vary Your Teaching Strategies

Wow! You got me! What, how, why? You caught me by surprise. Oh my!

It is human nature to be intrigued by "the element of surprise." **Students respond favorably to teachers who keep them intrigued, wondering what exciting thing will happen next.** Let's be clear, however, that I am referring to teaching strategies and not to classroom management strategies. Regarding routines and procedures in the classroom – how to enter the room, when to focus attention on the teacher, how to pass in papers, how to ask for permission to speak, what to do when there is a fire drill, etc. – there is no room for the *element of surprise*! These procedures should remain consistent, so as not to become confusing or chaotic. But regarding teaching strategies, spice it up. As the saying goes, "Variety is the spice of life." Successful teachers know this, and they use every opportunity to spice up their lessons and vary daily activities.

We can all recall sitting in classrooms where the only variety that we noticed was the change of the date on the calendar every day. It was the same old same old, day in and day out. We walked into class, we opened our textbooks, the teacher lectured, we took notes, and you know the rest of the routine. A middle school student, speaking to me about his favorite teacher, said, "What's really great about Mr. Carter's class is that we never know what to expect. Some days we walk into class and he's dressed as the character we'll be discussing. Other days, he's hurrying us into the room saying, 'You won't believe what I have in store for you today.' The man is so full of energy that we all seem to 'catch' it. He keeps us moving all the time. Some days he wears us out. It's always something different – not that old boring lecture stuff that we get from some of our other teachers. All the kids love him, and even the tough kids behave in his class."

I think you'll agree that this student's words say a lot. However, the icing on the cake was when a fifth-grade student described her "favorite" teacher and the importance of variety in teaching. She said, with a giant smile on her face, "Ms. Barton is like chicken, but the good kind." "What do you mean?" I asked. "Well, I'll tell you what the bad kind is first. With some teachers, going to their class is like eating plain old chicken, cooked the same way, every single day. Even if you like it at first, you get tired of eating chicken cooked the same way all the time. But in Ms. Barton's class, some days it's fried chicken, some days it's barbecued chicken, some days it's chicken soup, some days it's baked chicken, and some days it's chicken nuggets, but it's always cooked really well – and all the kids like it, so we eat a lot of it, and we never get tired of it because it always changes." "Wow!" I thought. "From the mouths of babes."

Students respond well to teachers who use variety in the classroom – where they never know what to expect on any given day. Variety doesn't have to be fancy and it doesn't have to be difficult. You simply have to change your lesson activities often so that your lessons don't look the same from one day to the next. Keep your students engaged and on the edge of their seats, always wondering what's coming next.

> ✔ **Ask Yourself:** Do I vary my teaching strategies by moving quickly from exciting explanations to inviting discussions to interesting hands-on learning activities to class projects to student demonstrations of skills, and so on? Do I realize how many ways there are to prepare chicken?

Tip 48
Do What's Best, Not What's Easiest

What's Best for My Students

Do I do what's best for my students or what's easiest for me?
For it's easier, yes, to sit at my desk and let each be his own busy bee,
But "busy work" becomes "dizzy work" and the students soon will resent it,
And as anyone knows, their frustration grows, and soon they will all need to vent it.
Yes, teaching takes work, and you simply can't shirk what's best for what's
*   unproblematic*
Because if you do, what's easiest for you will soon lead to all things erratic.
So choose what's best for your students, and never what's easiest for you,
For nothing worthwhile, such as reaching a child, will ever be easy to do!

It's not always easy to be positive, but being positive is best for your students. It would be easier to dole out *busy work,* but that's *not* what's best for your students. It is far easier to let the textbook tell you exactly what to teach as opposed to simply using the textbook as one of several references, but letting the textbook make your decisions is *not* what's best for your students. An objective test consisting only of multiple choice and true-false items is far easier for a teacher to grade than a more authentic form of assessment, but doing what's easy is not what's best for your students. Planning lessons that engage students continually is time consuming, but it is what's best for your students. Catching up on grading papers or answering e-mails while students work busily at their computer stations, on their tablets, etc. will give you more time to yourself later, but it's not what's best for your students. Teaching all students as if they were on the same level is far easier than teaching students at their individual levels, but it's *not* what's best for students. Learning about and maximizing available technology can be time consuming, but it's definitely what's best for students. Being professional at all costs is not always easy, but it is what's best for your students.

We're human, and it's often tempting to choose the path of least resistance. It's completely up to you to resist the path of least resistance and make all decisions based on what's best for your students, not what's easiest for you.

✔ **Ask Yourself:** When making any decision – in planning, in instructing, in dealing with behavior issues, or in making any professional decision – ask yourself this one question: Is this what's best for my students?

Tip 49
Get Out from Behind the Desk!

*There's something called a teacher's desk, and its purpose is for storage
It holds all your stuff so that when you need something, you know just
where to forage.*

There is a piece of furniture in every classroom known as the teacher's desk. If you are a new teacher, have you figured out the purpose of that piece of furniture? If not, I'll tell you. There are two main purposes for a teacher's desk:

1. to store stuff, and
2. to sit at when students are not in the room.

That's basically it. There are no other purposes for that piece of furniture. BUT, many teachers have never received that memo, and they actually sit at their desks while the students are in the room. Some practically LIVE there! That's a huge mistake. Here's why: A physical barrier promotes a mental barrier. It physically separates people, thus emotionally separating them. And the LAST thing you want is to be emotionally separated from your students. You want them to know that you are just like a coach, right in the game with them. (Please notice that there is never a coach's desk on the sideline of a football field.) Feel free to sit at your desk to do paperwork any time that the students are not present. But when the students are present, even when they are working independently, it is vital that you are *in the game* with them. As we have already discussed (see Tip 13), the closer you are in proximity to your students, the less likely they are to misbehave and the more likely they are to remain engaged in their studies. So get out from behind that desk. If, for some reason, you must occasionally sit while teaching, simply take your chair from behind your desk and put it right in the center of your students. (Rolling chairs work great for this.) This way, you are still "with" them, as opposed to physically separating yourself from them.

It's also important to remember not to sit behind your desk during parent or student conferences. Place your chair next to the parent or the student, thus removing any physical barrier.

> ✔ **Ask Yourself:** Do I use my desk as a "stuff holder" when my students are in the room and a personal workstation when students are not in the room?

Instruction: Section Highlights

◆ When you make a mistake – and you will – admit it, learn from it, recover quickly, and move on.

◆ Teach students at their level of understanding.

◆ Observe and learn from other teachers as often as possible.

◆ Remember that the one who does the "doing" is doing the learning.

◆ Remember that though textbooks can be valuable resources, you, the teacher, are the most valuable resource.

◆ Be a model of the behaviors you want your students to possess.

◆ Recognize and focus on the strengths of each of your students.

◆ Provide opportunities for students to work collaboratively.

◆ Relate the skills you teach to the lives and interests of your students.

◆ Keep abreast of and maximize the use of available technology.

◆ When you assign homework, make sure it is meaningful, doable, and quick.

◆ Model new skills for your students so that they can "see" what they will soon be able to do.

◆ Encourage student participation by engaging them in fun, interesting, meaningful activities, not passive sitting and listening.

◆ Challenge your students to explain, create, evaluate, analyze, and question.

◆ Assess students in a way that actually shows whether they possess the skills you have taught as opposed to whether they have memorized a set of notes.

◆ Provide variety in order to keep students wondering, guessing, and enjoying learning.

◆ Make decisions based on what's best for your students, not what's most convenient for you.

◆ Avoid putting physical barriers (like a teacher's desk) between you and your students.

Section Four
Professionalism

I Bleed Professionalism

I bleed professionalism, yet I don't need medical attention.

The blood is not the red kind, but the kind of another dimension –

A dimension where I am a role model, and my blood spills onto each student.

From me, I hope they will learn to be sensible, practical, prudent,

For everything I do and say is under their scrutiny

Because everything I do and say influences who they will be.

My co-workers watch me also – I'm under a microscope.

They wait to see just how I'll react in a tough situation and cope.

So I'm careful about my words, my dress, and the look upon my face.

One's professionalism or lack of it can make or break a place!

Tip 50
Maintain a Positive Reputation

Want to know who the best teachers in the school are?
ASK THE STUDENTS!

Every teacher, in every classroom, on every school campus has a *reputation.* **If you have taught for more than one week, you have a reputation.** Students quickly identify the caring teachers, the screamers, the ones who give the most homework, the ones who hold the record for office referrals, etc. Consider the fact that most parents never see their children's teachers teach. But almost all parents have an opinion about *how* their children's teachers teach. For the most part, parents judge the reputations of teachers based on what their children tell them. Teachers know the reputations of their counterparts also. **You do not have to observe a teacher in the classroom to make a fairly accurate determination of that teacher's character and effectiveness in the classroom.** You can watch teachers take their classes to lunch and tell whether management is in place. You can watch teachers interact with students on the school grounds and know what kind of rapport they do or don't share. You can walk down the hallways and know who's teaching. And you can listen to their conversations with others and learn a lot about their attitudes, their professionalism, and their overall effectiveness. Also – whether you want to or not – you will overhear students talking about their teachers.

No teacher wants to have a negative reputation, yet many do. So how do you avoid becoming one of the teachers with a negative reputation? **The best way to steer clear of a negative reputation is not to establish one in the first place** because once you have one, it's difficult to change it – not impossible, but difficult. But if you simply teach from your heart, treat your students with dignity, resist negativity, approach each day with hard work, dedication, and enthusiasm, and act professionally, you will be able to enjoy and DESERVE a positive reputation!

✔ **Ask Yourself:** Am I aware of my reputation with my students? Do they see me as a caring, enthusiastic, competent professional whose class they WANT to be in?

Tip 51
Steer Clear of the Blame Game

Who's to Blame?

The college professor said, "Such rawness in a student is a shame. Lack of preparation in high school is to blame."

Said the high school teacher, "Good heavens, that boy's a fool. The fault, of course, is with the middle school."

The middle school teacher said, "From stupidity may I be spared. They sent him in so unprepared."

The primary teacher huffed, "Kindergarten blockheads all. They call that preparation? Why, it's worse than none at all."

The kindergarten teacher said, "Such lack of training never did I see. What kind of woman must that mother be?"

The mother said, "Poor helpless child. He's not to blame. His father's people were all the same."

Said the father at the end of the line, "I doubt the rascal's even mine."

Anonymous

Any teacher, any parent, and any child can relate to "Who's to Blame." Why? Because we've all been guilty of it. But the simple fact is that playing the blame game does us no good. It does not move us forward, it does not help children, it does not improve teaching, and it wastes our valuable time and energy. There's only one piece of advice I can give you regarding the blame game: DON'T PARTICIPATE!

Every year, we receive a certain group of students. We do not get to "pick" them. We do not get to pick their parents. We do not have any say in their educational experiences prior to teaching them. We do, however, get to take them as they are and help them to grow from there. And don't forget that we DID pick our jobs and this profession. We filled out an application! So be careful not to let yourself fall prey to feeling victimized or engaging in the blame game – it's a lame game. It's a dangerous road that leads to frustration, anger, self-righteousness, and all that is negative and harmful, not only to you, but also to the students whose lives you influence daily.

✔ **Ask Yourself:** Have I ever found myself playing the blame game? If so, has it helped me or my students in any way?

Tip 52
Choose Your Reactions

If the students know they're getting to you, they're going to keep on trying.
You're selling your reactions, and every student is buying!

I believe that the BIGGEST mistake any teacher will ever make is one that many teachers make on a daily basis: We let students know when they *get to us*. **It's not our feelings that reveal who we are to others, but rather our actions.** And one of the most difficult tasks to accomplish as a teacher is the ability to control your actions and reactions and maintain your composure at all costs. **We often have very *little* control over our circumstances, but we have very *much* control over how we choose to react to those circumstances.**

In the classroom, students will work diligently at determining who you are as a person and a teacher. They are masters at reading adults. They are masters at pushing adults' buttons. They will try to make you stop, stare at the ceiling, and lose your patience. They will try to see if they can make you clench your teeth as you speak in an angry tone. They will even try to see how far they can make the vein stick out on the side of your neck! An important word of advice: Don't play the game. You will feel frustrated at times. That's normal. But to roll your eyes, clench your teeth when you speak, fold your arms and tap your foot as you stare at the ceiling, sigh, raise your voice, or exhibit any of the many signs of a loss of composure will only serve to let students know that you *did* play, you *did* lose, and you gave your control over to them.

Remember that you can be serious without looking angry. You can discipline a student in a thoughtful, professional manner. You just have to avoid ever letting them know they are getting to you personally. When students realize that you will not play the game and that you are truly a professional, they will stop trying to see how red they can make your face get, how far that vein in your neck will stick out. . . . You will, in turn, earn their respect, but most importantly, you will serve as the role model that many of them so desperately need.

I know a teacher who is always assigned the "problem" students. She teaches the ones no one else wants to teach due to their prior histories of misbehavior. But this teacher knows how to choose her reactions very carefully.

Each year, she welcomes the opportunity to teach the "unteachables." She treats them with dignity, patience, and respect. She has high expectations for all. Oh yes, they "try" her at first. It happens every year. But the fact that she never gives them the reactions they're seeking soon neutralizes them. When they realize that she will not lose her temper, that she will not stop believing in them, and that she will do anything to make them successful, they stop trying to provoke negative responses from her. It works every year, as her record has shown. And her influence on her students is nothing short of profound.

Remember, your circumstances will never *determine* who you are, but rather your reactions to circumstances will *reveal* who you are to students, parents, and co-workers. Choose your reactions!

✔ **Ask Yourself:** Do my students sometimes control my emotions? Do they know when they are aggravating me? If so, you can change that by being the "actor" you were hired to be. Pretend to be in control, even when you're not!

Tip 53
Don't Let Negative Co-workers Affect You

Mrs. WarnYa

On every single faculty, there lives a Mrs. WarnYa
Like a very heavy necklace, if you let her, she'll adorn ya.
She warns of all the troubled kids and bad administration.
She'll show you, if you'll listen, how to seek retaliation.
With bitterness, her nectar, and doom, her jubilation
She never seems to realize that her actual revelation
Is admitting she's a gossip, admitting she's a fake.
Befriending Mrs. WarnYa is always a mistake!

FACT: If there are more than three people on your school's faculty, then chances are good that there's a negative faction! This is not to suggest that the majority of teachers are negative individuals. They're not. But one negative individual can have a tremendous negative influence on other co-workers. To date, I have yet to find a faculty that has been spared of a Mrs. WarnYa.

As teachers, we all stand at a fork in the road where we are faced with a very important decision. We can choose to go "left" – fitting in and falling prey – or we can choose to go "right" – doing what's best for students: the only way! The fact is that you will not be alone on either path you choose. One way, however, is more difficult. It takes more guts. Which is that? The "right" way. Let's look at what you'll get on each path.

If you go "right" and do what's best for students, there are both pros and cons:

Pros: *Your classroom will be an exciting place, student achievement will rise, student self-esteem will rise, you will be highly respected by respectable educators, and your contribution to society will be immeasurable.*
Cons: *You will work hard, and you will run the risk of being scrutinized by the people who chose to go "left."*
Final destination: *You will be a happy, successful, hard-working, contributing, truly effective, highly qualified, and highly respected teacher who touches lives and makes a difference.*

If you go "left" and choose to fit in and fall prey, there are also pros and cons:

> **Pros**: *All the negative people will like you, you will be allowed to gripe all you want, and your workload will be lightened by the overuse of worksheets, busy work, and time fillers. Also, you will experience the bliss of denial by simply blaming society, parents, administration, and students, conveniently forgetting that you have control, with very few exceptions, over what goes on in your classroom.*
>
> **Cons**: *You will very likely struggle with management and discipline, but it will at least give you something more to gripe about. You will know all the latest gossip, your cynical attitude will breed resentment in students, respectable educators will have no respect for you, and last, but definitely not least, you may figure out one day that you've taken the wrong road, and you'll be sorry.*
>
> **Final destination**: *You will find yourself a burned out, cynical, bitter individual who missed out on all the rewards of teaching and touching lives.*

The choice seems obvious, but remember that the main difference between truly effective and truly ineffective teachers lies in the choices they have made along the way. Make the "right" choice! And remember that you can be kind to Mrs. WarnYa without agreeing with her. When she complains about a student, you can respond by saying, "I love that kid!" When she warns you about a student she taught whom you will now be teaching, you can say, "I can tell you're concerned about him. I'll keep you posted on his progress." (More about this in Tip 101.)

✔ **Ask Yourself:** After reading this tip, have I already identified who, on my own faculty, has chosen which path? And am I aligning myself with those on the path I've chosen while still being kind to (but not enabling) those who have chosen the other path?

Tip 54
Learn to Work Effectively with Parents

> **Please, Teacher**
>
> *Please, teacher, treat my child as if he were your own.*
> *For if you do, I'm more likely to*
> *Answer when you phone,*
> *More likely to work beside you, less likely to cause you woe.*
> *I've sent you the best that I have to offer, and to me, he's great. Don't you know?*

One of the biggest fears of new teachers is dealing with parents – namely the angry ones. And, **if a new teacher does not know a few simple tricks for working cooperatively with parents, parent conferences can be frustrating and downright frightening experiences.** So read on if you would like to learn ways to work cooperatively with parents – even the angry ones.

As I walked down the hall of a high school, I met up with a new teacher who was in tears. I asked what was wrong, and she answered, "I'm on my way to call a parent who's really upset with me, and I don't know how to defend myself against her." "Why is she upset with you?" I asked. "Well, we sent out letters to invite parents to come in for private conferences. This parent claims she never got the letter, but I know I mailed all of them." "Okay," I said. "I'm going to walk you through this. First of all, let's capitalize on the very positive fact that this parent cares enough about her child's education to want to come to a conference." "I never thought about it that way," said the new teacher. I then told her exactly what to say during the phone conversation. Here are the instructions I gave her:

- Begin by saying, "I understand that you're very upset about not receiving a letter regarding the parent conferences. And I just want you to know that I was very impressed with the fact that you cared enough about your son to want to come to school and meet with his teacher. That says a lot about you as a parent."
- Then say, "I'm so sorry that you didn't receive the letter. But I'm anxious to meet with you, and I'm willing to do my best to accommodate your schedule."
- Next, ask, "When would be a convenient time for us to meet?"

Notice that nothing in the aforementioned conversation was in any way defensive. That's important, because when parents are angry, teachers often make the mistake of engaging in the struggle and arguing with them. What they should really do is allow the parent to express his or her concerns, remaining calm and professional throughout. You see, **when a person is angry, the anger can only last so long, unless, of course, the other party is fueling it.** If the other party remains calm and does not become defensive, the angry parent will soon run out of steam. That's the opportunity to begin solving the problem.

Anyway, the new teacher went into the office to make the phone call and I waited out in the hall. About five minutes later, she walked out of the office beaming. She said to me, "It's like we're best friends now! She and I really hit it off after I complimented her on her genuine concern for her son. We're meeting tomorrow."

Yes, sometimes it really can be that simple. Approach all parents with the assumption that they truly do want what's best for their children, and work cooperatively and professionally with them in helping to achieve a common goal. Listen to them when they are upset, let them blow off steam if necessary, and then establish the fact that you're anxious to work cooperatively with them to solve the problem. Also, try to ensure that your comments about a student include his or her strengths. Make it a practice to establish positive communication with parents up front, and then when the occasional negative situation occurs, they will be much more willing to work cooperatively with you in solving the problem. Setting up a class webpage is a wonderful way to allow parents to get to know you and remain abreast of what's going on in your classroom.

A parent is much more likely to support you when he believes you are genuinely interested in his child. If he has received several positive notes, calls, texts, or e-mails from you in the past, he's going to be convinced that you're on the side of his child. Whether he has ever responded to those contacts is not the point. If the first contact he ever receives from you is negative, he's much more likely to feel that you are on the opposing team, thus prompting him to take a defensive stand.

Remember that even if a parent walks out of a conference disagreeing with you, make sure that he or she walks out knowing that you acted professionally and did not lose your cool. You may not be able to control an angry parent's reactions, but you can most certainly control your own reactions in every such situation.

> ✔ **Ask Yourself:** Do I make a concerted effort to establish positive communication with the parents of my students? Do the parents of my students view me as a teammate or an opponent?

Tip 55
Participate in After-school Functions

> **She Cheered for Me**
>
> *There must be some type of crazy malfunction,*
> *For my teacher was at my after-school function.*
> *I thought that she lived in her classroom at school.*
> *Did they let her out? 'Cause it's extremely cool*
> *That she cared enough to come to the game.*
> *She cheered for me, so for her I'll do the same!*

We all have lives of our own outside of our classrooms. If you're a new teacher, then you're the exception. (Just kidding – but I know it feels as if you don't have a life outside of school right now!) Whenever possible, however, it is important to participate in after-school functions. I'll share a personal experience here. When I was in third grade, my sisters, a couple of friends, and I invited my third-grade teacher, Mrs. Robichaux, to a talent show we were planning. Little did we dream that she would actually attend. In fact, we were so convinced that she wouldn't come that we never got around to planning the talent show. But she showed up! We went into a panic, because we had nothing planned. We quickly hung a sheet outside on an old clothes-line – our curtain – seated Mrs. Robichaux in a chair, and huddled behind the curtain to come up with something, anything! Thank goodness that my younger sister, Andrée, loved to perform. We kept sending her out to entertain Mrs. Robichaux. She first sang "Leaving on a Jet Plane." Mrs. Robichaux clapped enthusiastically, and Andrée returned to us behind the curtain. We then sent her out to exhibit her gymnastic abilities. The poor little thing, who was only 6 years old at the time, was exhausted. But each time we sent her out, Mrs. Robichaux acted as though it was the most amazing talent she had ever witnessed. Then we all came out, took a bow, and Mrs. Robichaux left. In retrospect, I'm sure that Mrs. Robichaux knew, after the first act, that we had nothing prepared. But she never let on. She never even commented on the fact that the only participant in the talent show was my little sister. The following day, she thanked us for inviting her and said how much she had enjoyed herself. And we realized how much Mrs. Robichaux cared. She gave of her own time, after school hours, to watch a six year old turn cartwheels across the yard. Is that dedication or what?

Participation in after-school functions sends a message to students and to parents that you care. You do have your own life and you cannot possibly attend every after-school function that your students participate in. But here's what you can do – you can set aside maybe an hour or two a week to attend one of these functions. If it's a ball game, you don't have to stay for the entire game. Show up, say hello, watch a few plays, and then leave. If you can't physically attend a function, ask students about it the next day. That, in itself, will go a long way toward showing that you care. But be involved and interested – even if you can't attend.

In our case, our mother was not happy with us when she learned of what we had put poor Mrs. Robichaux through. However, she was definitely impressed with the fact that Mrs. Robichaux had not only endured, but pretended to enjoy our "talent" show. Parents who believe that you care about their children will be much more likely to support you and work cooperatively with you. Students who believe that you care about them will work harder, will behave better, and will even "turn cartwheels" for you! As the saying goes, "Students won't care how much you know until they know how much you care."

PS: Andrée went on to receive a Master's degree in the Performing Arts. We believe Mrs. Robichaux's unbridled enthusiasm and encouragement had something to do with it!

✔ **Ask Yourself:** Do I take an interest in my students' after-school interests by occasionally attending their functions or at least asking about them (and making a big deal over them) when I cannot attend?

Tip 56
Use Social Networking Appropriately

It's the ABUSE, not the USE, of social networking that should be avoided.

Social networking – it's how anyone can connect with everyone anywhere and everywhere at any time. It provides a platform for instant news, instant communication with friends and family, instant alerts, instant publishing of thoughts, ideas, and information, and instant learning about or sharing of any topic you can possibly imagine. You can appropriately "post" or make someone's reputation toast. You can properly blog or improperly flog. You can "friend" or you can offend. Your choice does not really lie in whether to use social networking but in HOW to use it, especially now that you are a teacher, a role model, a professional.

The following are a few tips for ensuring that you are using social networking appropriately:

- Know that the opportunities for connecting with other educators from around the globe and using online professional development opportunities are endless, thanks to social networking. So please don't avoid it. Just avoid using it inappropriately.

- Familiarize yourself, immediately, with your school's policy for the use of social media for teachers and for students. Follow that policy to the letter.

- Provide students with clear guidelines for your classroom's (and school's) social networking policy. Continually remind them about appropriate vs. inappropriate use of social networking in your classroom.

- Set up a class page to post classroom news, school news, assignment due dates, announcements, etc. Allow your students to help in maintaining and updating the class page.

- Connect with other educators and chat about research, trends, techniques, lesson planning, classroom management, etc.

- Connect your students with other classrooms around the globe and learn from one another.

- Make use of privacy settings, and be sure to keep your personal social networking activity separate from your professional social networking activity.
- Don't include your students as part of your personal social networking group.
- Remember that even privacy settings are not always foolproof, so be very careful about anything you post on social media sites.
- Just act responsibly. Don't post anything online that could jeopardize your job or your reputation if anyone and everyone viewed it.

Yes, it's true that some teachers have lost their jobs because of inappropriate activity on social media sites. There are also teachers who have lost their jobs for a plethora of reasons that had nothing to do with social media. Social networking is not the problem. Inappropriate behavior is the problem. You WANT to be a connected educator. But remember that posting something online is like posting the same thing on a billboard on the side of the freeway. The real difference is that when you post something on your favorite social media site, chances are good that more people will view it than would view the billboard!

✔ **Ask Yourself:** Now that I am a teacher, do I approach social networking responsibly? Am I careful not to post anything that would be embarrassing if my students, their parents, or my superintendent read it?

Tip 57
Avoid Lounge Gossip

By swallowing evil words unsaid, no one has ever yet harmed his stomach.
—Winston Churchill

Have you been warned yet to stay away from the teachers' lounge? Have you heard that that's where the gossips gather? Whether they gather in the lounge or elsewhere, they are usually present in every school. It's sad, because most teachers are genuinely good people. I've always believed that any teacher gossiping about students does not realize that **gossip serves one purpose: it HARMS!**

A wonderful benefit for both teachers and students is the fact that we have the advantage of being able to start over every year. Imagine if you, as a teacher, would continue to be evaluated by your administrator based on previous mistakes you have made in your teaching, or in your life, for that matter. Many of us would be doomed before we even began a new year. But sadly, many students are "doomed" each year because of the careless, harmful words spoken about them between teachers. If you are a teacher, you will encounter others, somewhere along the way, who will try to engage with you in empty, meaningless gossip. Do not participate. Not only is it unprofessional, but it symbolizes the antithesis of what we truly stand for: serving and helping others. If you can't say something nice about someone, don't say anything.

And please don't stay away from the lounge. You need and deserve an occasional break. I encourage you to go into the lounge every chance you get and be the most positive person there. Enlist the support of several of your positive co-workers and go into the lounge each day on a mission – to speak only of positive things about your life, about your students, about education, about anything. Just be sure it's positive. Soon, the negative people will be so uncomfortable that they'll leave, and the lounge will become a positive, gossip-free zone. It's time for the positive teachers to take their lounges back!

> ✔ **Ask Yourself:** Knowing that my words tell the world who I really am, do I make every effort to avoid any conversations that belittle my students, my co-workers, students' parents, or this profession I have chosen?

Tip 58
Enlist the Support of Others

I can do things you cannot, you can do things I cannot; together we can do great things.

—Mother Teresa

We try to instill in our students that teamwork – cooperating and collaborating – is important – it's important in winning a game, it's important in accomplishing a task, and it's important in solidifying a community. We teach our students to ask for help when they need it. We teach them to help others when others are in need. We teach them that in order to succeed, they must be team players. As a teacher said to me, "I'm not a one-man show. I enlist the support of anyone who can provide assistance in helping my students to learn." This was a high school teacher who had his students help him in decorating the room, gathering materials for activities, and just about anything else with which he needed help. He often had community members serving as guest speakers in his classroom. A group of volunteer parents were regularly in his classroom assisting with a multitude of tasks. And he even had other teachers coming in to demonstrate techniques for the benefit of both him and his students. He was a mentor to a new teacher, and he claimed that he got more new and innovative ideas from the new teacher than from any other member on the staff. "I believe in teamwork," he said. "When you get everyone involved, not only does it keep your classroom interesting, but it lets parents feel like active participants in their children's education. It also allows for community involvement, which is beneficial to all." His science project demonstrations were always the *hit* of the year, and he invited everyone to attend. "Anyone is welcome in our classroom. But I'm warning you, if you walk in, we'll put you to work."

Not only was this teacher willing to enlist the support of others in the education of his students, but the students also went into the community to volunteer their time in assisting others. "It's a reciprocal kind of thing," he said. "We accept assistance from others, and we give something back. I think the most surprising thing to many is that so many people – colleagues, administrators, parents, community members, etc. – are so willing to help. All you have to do is ask!"

✔ **Ask Yourself:** Do I teach my students (and model for them) the importance of working together? Do I seize every opportunity to instill in them the importance of community?

Tip 59
Be the Best You Can Be

Success comes from knowing that you did your best to become the best that you are capable of becoming.

—John Wooden

There is little in life that gives us more satisfaction than knowing that we have done something and given it our best. Teaching offers us that opportunity every day. **No teacher is perfect.** All teachers make mistakes. (Hey, new teachers, we veterans are still learning to teach, so we still make lots of mistakes. But the best teachers try not to make the same mistakes twice.) Despite the fact that we do make mistakes – lots of them – teachers who give their best every day are the ones who touch lives. In teaching, even the most difficult days can be successful ones when we are resolved to give it our all. In fact, the most difficult days are often the most rewarding ones – those days when we are truly put to the test. There will be days when you are not feeling well, either emotionally or physically, but if you choose to come to school you must be at your best. There will be days when students test your patience because they do not understand what you're trying to teach. Again, try a new way of explaining it and do not give into frustration. There will be times when students test your resolve because they're just being kids and are doing things they should not be doing. That's why they need adults in their lives. There will be days when you are feeling overwhelmed and are tempted to *throw in the towel*. Do not give up, and do not give in. Rather, give it all you've got – and then some.

It is only in giving our best that we can possibly expect to bring out the best in our students. It is important that they see both our successes and our struggles. It is important that they realize that they will succeed and struggle. It is important that they understand that all any of us can do is to give everything we do our very best.

So don't beat yourself up when you make mistakes, when your day doesn't go exactly as you had planned, when you are challenged with unanticipated obstacles at work. Just be the best teacher you can be, and your rewards will come to you in the form of young lives forever changed because of your influence and example.

> ✔ **Ask Yourself:** Am I committed to giving my very best to my students and being the best teacher I can be, even on difficult days? If so, even on your worst days, you should sleep like a baby – waking up and crying every two hours! Kidding.

Tip 60
Set Goals for Your Own Improvement

Which Way?

I stood at a fork in the road
And didn't know which way to go
But since I had no destination in mind
If I got there, I'd never know!

FACT: Written goals are far more likely to be accomplished than mental goals. Most people have goals, lots of them. But many people never accomplish them. Consider New Year's resolutions. "I'm going to get skinny." "I'm going to save more money." "I'm going to get rid of the clutter in my house." "I'm going to be a nicer person." Notice how vague these goals are. There's no real plan of action, so they usually aren't accomplished. It would be far more "doable" to say, "I'm going to walk 20 minutes a day, three days a week." "I'm going to increase my monthly contributions to my savings by 5%." "I'm going to have a garage sale to get rid of things around the house that I don't need." "I'm going to make a special effort to do something nice for someone, just one thing, every day." And then you write them down and keep them in a place where you will see them daily. Goals are accomplished one step at a time. And written goals are much more likely to be accomplished than non-written ones!

In the classroom, you might say, "I'm going to learn to use *[insert newest technological device]* this month so that I can utilize it in my teaching." "I'm going to devise a new classroom management plan and implement it consistently." "I'm going to include student-oriented activities in my lesson plans daily."

Whatever your goals, write them down and post them. Take one step toward your goals every day, and you'll eventually reach your destination. Don't just stand at the fork in the road scratching your head. In the words of Mark Twain:

The secret of getting ahead is getting started. The secret of getting started is breaking your complex overwhelming tasks into small manageable tasks, and then starting on the first one.

✔ **Ask Yourself:** What are three goals I'd like to accomplish – one for this week, one for this month, and one for this school year? Write them down, and get started accomplishing them.

Tip 61
Be Flexible

Blessed are the flexible, for they shall not be bent out of shape!
—Anonymous (Gumby, maybe?)

Any teacher will tell you that in teaching there are both predictabilities and unpredictabilities. Prepare yourself for some of the following unpredictabilities:

◆ Unannounced emergency drills.

◆ Unexpected intercom announcements.

◆ Students getting sick.

◆ Unexpected discipline challenges.

◆ Unanticipated student questions.

◆ Schedule changes.

◆ Knocks at the classroom door.

◆ Unannounced observations by administration.

◆ Running out of time to teach a particular skill.

◆ Overestimating the time it will take to teach a particular skill.

◆ Policy changes.

◆ Technology changes.

◆ Curriculum changes.

◆ Changes in teaching assignments, and so on and so on and so on . . .

The only real predictability in teaching is the fact that it is unpredictable. Get accustomed to it. Don't let yourself get bent out of shape by things over which you have no control. And realize that many things are going to be out of your control. Be flexible. If you don't learn to bend, you'll eventually break! So choose to bend rather than break, and roll with the punches, for sanity's sake!

✔ **Ask Yourself:** Do I like everything to go as I have it planned in my mind? Does my mind get a little frazzled when one of teaching's many unpredictabilities disrupts my plan? Do I realize that effective teachers are much more like elastic than like plastic?

Tip 62
Ask Lots of Questions

> **Too Many Questions**
>
> *You say I ask too many questions, but you just don't seem to see*
> *That I wonder about so many things for which answers there surely must be.*
> *But once I know an answer, a new question grows in my mind*
> *Because what I learn uncovers new problems with answers to find.*
> *So be patient with my questioning; there still is so much I don't know*
> *But I do know that learning more answers will certainly help me to grow.*

New teachers are often afraid to ask questions. Said a new teacher, "I have so many questions, but I don't know whom to ask. I'm afraid to look stupid, so I can't ask other teachers. They'll probably think I should know these things. Then my reputation will suffer. But I need answers!" Sadly, this is a very typical concern of new teachers. They're afraid to ask for fear of appearing incompetent.

This is what new teachers need to know:

◆ Teaching is not an exact science, so all teachers should remain in a state of questioning.

◆ Teachers, in general, are more than willing to share their techniques, ideas, and philosophies with each other.

◆ Asking questions does not make you appear incompetent. Rather, it makes you look like a dedicated professional who wants to do what's best for students.

◆ True professionals will not sacrifice learning something new for fear of appearing ignorant. We are all ignorant when it comes to teaching. There's so much we don't yet know.

If you want to be an effective teacher, you can't afford NOT to ask questions. **Any teacher, regardless of years of experience, who does not question will stagnate.** So ask lots of questions – of your co-workers, of your professional learning communities, of your colleagues on social networking sites, of your students, and of yourself. Just be prepared for the fact that every time you get one question answered, it will open a whole new world of possibilities, for which you'll have more questions, which will, of course, lead to more answers, which will then awaken new questions, which will require more answers. Any questions?

> ✔ **Ask Yourself:** What are three teaching-related questions I would like to have answered? Go out today and get those questions answered.

Tip 63
Dress Like a Professional

Students will judge you, partly, by your dress
When you don't look like a professional, they will respect you less.

If you walked through a crowded airport, you would instantly be able to spot pilots and flight attendants because they are professionally dressed in uniform. That is because when you step onto an airplane, you want to feel like you are in capable, competent hands. But wouldn't the pilot be just as capable and competent if he were dressed in flip-flops and jeans? Yes, but the passengers would not view him that way. So the uniforms are intentional.

If you walked into a courtroom, could you spot the attorneys? Consider this: If you were accused of a crime that you did not commit, and on the day of your trial your attorney arrived in gym clothes, you would immediately think, "I'm going to jail." Not because the attorney is less competent, but because the jurors, the ones who will determine your fate, would not take him seriously.

It has been proven, time and again, that **the way we dress influences the way others perceive us**. So let's take this into a school. There they are – hundreds of anxious, perceptive, role-model-seeking students waiting to form perceptions of their teachers. And here come the teachers. How are they dressed? That depends. A sad fact is that you could not walk into most schools and immediately spot all of the teachers based on their professional attire. Some you would recognize, instantly, as teachers. Others would be dressed in way-too-casual attire. Does that make them less competent? No. But it does change the way their students perceive them, which affects their effectiveness!

Teaching is the noblest profession of all. So why don't all teachers dress the part? So should you go out, on your meager salary, and buy expensive clothing? No. But you should not dress like your students, like you're going to the gym, or like you're going to a ball game. If you're going to be on your feet all day, don't expect to wear high heels. Professional attire does not have to be uncomfortable. It just has to make you look like a proud, respectful, competent professional!

✔ **Ask Yourself:** Here's a question to ask yourself before you leave for work each day: "If a stranger were to meet me on the street, would he know that I am some type of professional on my way to work?" If your answer is yes, then you are dressed professionally. If not, then go back to your closet and change – quickly – before the students see you!

Tip 64
Devise a "Teacher Report Card"

If I, as your teacher, am allowed to grade you
Then why not allow you to grade me, too?

Want to know how you're REALLY doing as a teacher? Ask your students.

During my third year of teaching, I read, in a magazine for teachers, about the idea of a "teacher report card." I thought to myself, "My students receive report cards, yet they never get the opportunity to evaluate me, to tell me how *I'm* doing as their teacher." I loved the idea, though I must admit that it was a bit frightening, knowing that my students would be brutally honest with me. But who better to judge my effectiveness than my own students? They were my *clients*. I was there to serve them. Why shouldn't they be allowed to provide me with feedback as to how I was doing? I implemented the idea immediately, and the students loved it. They were a little amazed at the fact that they were actually going to get to "grade" their teacher.

The report card was simple and to the point. It had no space for the student's name, as the best way to get honest feedback from students is to allow them to express themselves anonymously. Questions and prompts included the following:

- Does my teacher make class interesting? If not, what could she do to make the class more interesting?
- Does my teacher care about me as a person?
- Does my teacher hold me accountable for my actions?
- Am I allowed to contribute my opinions in this class?
- Does my teacher allow me to actively participate in each lesson?
- Does my teacher treat all students fairly and with dignity and respect?
- Am I successful in this class? If not, what could my teacher do to help me to become more successful?
- Does my teacher enjoy teaching?
- Do I feel that my teacher is the best teacher she can be?
- What I like about this class is _____.

- What I do not like about this class is _____.
- If I could change one thing about this class, it would be _____.

Each time my students received their report cards, I also received mine. And I can tell you that it was the most useful and honest feedback that I ever received about my teaching.

Allowing your students to "grade" your performance accomplishes several things:

- It holds you, as their teacher, accountable.
- It gives a message to students that their opinions matter.
- It shows students that their input is valued.
- It keeps you on your toes!

Over the years, as I have shared this idea with teachers of all grade levels and content areas, I have continued to notice that good teachers love the idea and can't wait to implement it. Less effective teachers are less than enthusiastic about the idea of having their students grade them.

Be the most effective teacher you can be, and allow your students to help you become just that. Devise your own teacher report card, and allow your students to provide you with valuable feedback. They will!

> ✔ **Ask Yourself:** Do I want to get honest, useful feedback about my teaching? Is the idea of a "teacher report card" a little scary? If I allow my students to tell me how I'm doing, what's the worst that can happen? What's the best?

Tip 65
Be a Role Model for Your Students

Students are looking at all that you do.
They watch, and then they emulate you!

When we sign a contract and call ourselves "teacher," we accept the profound responsibility of being a role model for every one of our students. Students need role models, and they seek them out in their lives. **Think back to your own role models. We all had them (and are hopefully still finding more). They were the people who cared about you, who encouraged your success, who inspired you to accomplish – people who possessed qualities that you wanted to emulate.** I often remind teachers that the students watch them very closely, and that their actions, of course, speak much louder than their words. As teachers, we often forget just how loudly our actions speak, and we end up modeling the exact opposites of the lessons we're trying to teach our students. It looks something like this:

Teacher yells at a student: "Don't you yell at me, young lady!"
Teacher, with a very unpleasant look, says to a belligerent student: "Take that look off of your face!"

These are actual scenarios of teachers modeling the exact behaviors they are trying to prevent in students! You see, students notice everything. Isn't it true that they notice when you wear a new outfit, when you get a haircut, when you NEED a haircut, when you are not feeling well, when you change your cologne or perfume? And isn't it true that they notice if you treat one student in a more favorable way than other students???

Just in case you are not convinced of how closely your students watch your actions, here is a challenge for you. Walk into your classroom tomorrow and ask, "Would any of you like to imitate me?" They'll imitate you, and they'll do it well! They can walk like you, they can talk like you, they can teach like you, and yes, they can even handle conflict like you. Remember that students may not always do what you say, but they notice everything you do!

> **Ask Yourself:** Since I know that my students are watching everything I do, which behaviors do I want them to see and emulate, and which would I prefer them not to see and emulate?

Tip 66
Cooperate with Administration

The keystone of successful business is cooperation. Friction retards progress.
—*James Cash (J.C.) Penney*

I often hear teachers complaining about their administrators. I usually listen for a while and then ask, "What percentage of the school day do you typically spend in your classroom with your students?" The answer is usually about 90%. Then I ask, "What percentage of the day do you spend in the presence of your administrator?" The answer is usually 1% or less, unless, of course, the teacher is married to his or her administrator, and since I'm not a marriage counselor, I leave immediately! The fact remains that some teachers spend a good percentage of their time complaining about someone they hardly see. Wouldn't it make more sense to put 100% of your efforts into the people with whom you spend more than 90% of your school day?

It will never happen that all of the teachers agree with administrative decisions all of the time. If you feel strongly about a particular issue, then you should discuss it privately and professionally with your administrator. But if the issue is one over which you have no control, let it go. I once knew a teacher who spent a considerable amount of her time griping about the dress code policy. She wanted to wear jeans, and the policy forbade it. She allowed that one issue to consume her. In anger, she turned against the administrator and refused to support any of his decisions. This, of course, was unprofessional. It affected her entire personality, so the students suffered also. (J.C. Penney, in his quote above, was right!)

In a truly effective school, teachers work together in cooperation with administration. They don't always agree with administration, yet they support administrative decisions, as much as possible, for the betterment of the school and ultimately the students. When they express their disagreements, they do it privately and professionally.

Don't get caught up in petty issues that lead to breakdowns in communication and cooperation. Remember, as discussed in Tip 69, to focus on what you CAN change – not on what you CAN'T. When we focus our efforts on working cooperatively toward a common goal – helping students – we may not always agree, but our students will always benefit.

✔ **Ask Yourself:** Do I do my best to cooperate with my school administrators? When I disagree with an administrator and want to voice my opinions, do I approach it professionally and come to the table with ideas for solutions?

Tip 67
Avoid "Acting When Angry"

No one should find it curious
That if you act when you are furious,
Anger is what you'll send out
And anger is what you'll get.
What you do out of anger is exactly
What you will eventually regret!

We've all been there. We can remember the feeling of boiling blood pulsing through our veins, building, racing through our bodies, and then – BANG – an explosion! We got angry, and we lost control. We said things that, to this day, we still regret. How we wish we could take it all back. But we can't. And the bad news is that we've probably all been guilty of not learning a lesson from it. We get angry again, and we act or speak without thinking. Once again, we lament the fact that we allowed ourselves to give in to the anger. We are all human; we all have emotions; we all experience anger. But not everyone expresses anger in the same way. As stated in Tip 52, **our feelings don't determine how others perceive us, but our actions surely do.**

A teacher stood in front of her class and "warned" her students several times to stop talking. They would stop for a few minutes, and then the talking would resume. Since I was seated in the back of the room, I watched her getting angrier with each warning. Her face became redder, her breathing became labored, her body became tense, and finally, she exploded. She threw her book down and began screaming. She then went into a tirade that she later regretted. But she couldn't take it back.

We often hear it suggested that when angry, we should *count to 10* or do something to calm ourselves down in order to avoid saying or doing something we'll later regret. Anger is a very powerful emotion. And in the classroom, it can be a very dangerous emotion if we do not control it. Just as we try to teach students to recognize their anger for what it is and to avoid losing control, so must we, as their teachers and role models, model appropriate ways of dealing with difficult situations. It is never appropriate to lose control of your emotions in the classroom. **When you're so angry that**

you can't think straight, you're right – you can't think straight. Wait until you can, and think about how you will handle the situation from a logical perspective.

> ✔ **Ask Yourself:** Am I always in control of my emotions in the classroom, or are my emotions sometimes in control of me?

Tip 68
Do Not Allow Your Personal Problems to Spill Over into the Classroom

FACT: If you do not have personal problems, then you are not a person. However, if you allow your personal problems to spill over into your classroom, then you are not a professional.

I once heard a teacher announce to her class, "Look, I'm having a bad day. I've been up all night with a sick child, so I'm not in a good mood. I'm going to try to concentrate on my teaching, but I'm tired. Also, we've fallen way behind in this chapter, so we're going to have to move fast today. Stay in your seats, and don't mess with me!"

Now imagine an airline pilot in a similar situation. "This is your pilot speaking, and boy, am I having a bad day! I've been up all night with a sick child, so I'm not in a good mood. I'm going to try to get you to New York, but I'm tired, so I'm not promising you anything. Also, we've fallen way behind on our schedule, so we're going to have to fly extra fast! So sit in your seats, and don't mess with me!"

What would you do as a passenger on this plane? You'd deplane, immediately, even in mid-flight! The fact is that students don't have the luxury of getting out of your classroom. However, they would feel the same way, in your classroom, that you would feel on that flight. Teachers are human, and so it is normal for them to experience human trials and tribulations. What is not normal is to allow those struggles to affect their students.

I'm sure that somewhere out there, there are pilots who are not having the best of days. The trick is never to allow their bad days to affect their passengers. And so it should be in the classroom. **Students are not vents for our frustrations.** If you're having a day that is so bad that you feel you cannot teach, then stay home. If you choose to come to school, however, be a professional! All "passengers" in your classroom should enjoy a safe flight and an on-time arrival.

✔ **Ask Yourself:** When I'm dealing with challenging personal issues, am I careful to keep those issues (and their resulting moods) out of my classroom and away from my students?

Tip 69
Focus on What You CAN Change

Try to control what's uncontrollable and soon you will be inconsolable!

Okay, so your administrator does not always see things the way you see them. Maybe the school's cafeteria food will never be classified as gourmet, the school custodian may miss a spot or two on occasion, and parents may not rear their children in ways that meet with your standards. But what does that have to do with what goes on within the four walls of your classroom? Very little, if anything. The fact is that **many people spend most of their time focusing on things they simply cannot change.** As teachers, we must learn to channel 100% of our energies into things we can do something about. And we can absolutely do something about the teaching and learning that takes place in our classrooms every day. The following are examples of teachers focusing needless energy on things they can do very little about:

- "I met Brandon's parents yesterday, and now I understand why he's like he is. He doesn't stand a chance."
- "Why is our principal insisting that we attend yet another in-service?"
- "Did you hear what Mrs. _____ told her students today?"
- "How can they expect us to teach from this textbook?"
- "Have you noticed the way that Mr. _____ looks at Ms. _____ ? I think there's something going on."
- "Kids today are just not what they used to be."
- "How I wish I had my time in. I'd retire today."

All right, I think you get the point. Surely you've heard this kind of talk in your own school. Negativity breeds negativity, misery loves company, water seeks its own level, and fill in whatever other clichéd expression that fits. The point is that none of it is good for you, and none of it is good for students.

> ✔ **Ask Yourself:** When faced with a problem at school, ask yourself, "Is there anything I can do to remedy this situation? If so, what's my plan of action?" If there's really nothing you can do, then let it go. If there is something you can do, then DO something!

Tip 70
Grow as a Professional

The day you're finished learning to teach is the day you should retire.

I've often heard it said that some teachers teach 30 years, and others teach one year 30 times! Education is like the field of medicine. We are constantly discovering new and more effective ways of doing things. Being in the classroom of a teacher who resists change and basically hasn't learned anything new in 20 years is like being operated on by a surgeon who resists change and hasn't learned anything new in 20 years.

*A superintendent told me that he requires ALL of his 2000 teachers to write professional growth plans, every year. These plans include the teachers' yearly goals for improvement. The plans are monitored and are then evaluated at the end of the year. "This ensures that ALL of my teachers are constantly getting better," he said, "We don't expect perfection, but we insist on improvement." When asked about why the goals were written and evaluated, he said, "**It's a fact that people who have specific written goals are far more successful than those who have vague mental goals.** That's why we also have district-wide goals, and they're posted in every classroom. We have a definite direction, and everyone is headed that way." When I asked a teacher in this district about her professional growth plan, she responded, "I wasn't crazy about the idea at first. It seemed like just one more thing we had to do, and I already had plenty enough to do. But having these goals keeps me sharp. I set them, and then I move toward them. And I always arrive at my destination a much more competent teacher."*

With the help of technology, we now have more opportunities to grow as professionals than ever. Participate in professional learning communities in both your school and online. Read blogs, watch webinars, and attend every training session you can possibly attend. There's no such thing as an overqualified teacher – just as I'm fairly sure there's no such thing as an overqualified surgeon!

> ✔ **Ask Yourself:** Am I connecting with fellow educators, reading, observing, trying new techniques, asking lots of questions, and receiving as much training as I can in order to continue learning to teach?

Professionalism: Section Highlights

- Maintain a positive reputation by being a consummate professional.
- Remember that though you cannot always control your circumstances, you CAN always control your reactions to those circumstances.
- Approach all parents with the assumption that they want what's best for their children. Make every effort to involve them and to work cooperatively with them.
- Show interest in your students' interests and attend after-school functions when possible.
- Don't avoid social networking. Use it. Just use it responsibly.
- Avoid any negative chatter, idle gossip, and the people who thrive on them.
- Enlist the support of community members, volunteer parents, students, and anyone else you can recruit in order to improve teaching and learning and instill a sense of community and teamwork.
- Set specific (written) goals for your own professional improvement.
- Be more "elastic" than "plastic" and learn to be more flexible.
- Don't be afraid to ask questions for fear of appearing incompetent.
- Dress in a way that shows you are a proud professional.
- Allow your students to evaluate your teaching with a "teacher report card."
- Always act in a way that you would be proud to have your students emulate.
- Work cooperatively and professionally with administration.
- Avoid doing or saying anything when you are angry. Calm down, think, and then act.
- Never allow your personal problems to affect your professional life.
- Learn something new about teaching and learning every day.

Section Five

Motivation and Rapport

Teacher, When You Lit a Spark in Me . . .

Teacher, when you lit a spark in me, my very best you soon did see
And once I was convinced that you cared, I worked much harder and I even dared
To scale the obstacles I used to avoid
For fear that my pride would be destroyed
I learned, from you, that I could do it
You challenged me and saw me through it
And when I fell, you lifted me
With your clever ways, you gifted me
With the knowledge that falling was a step to success
And at times, I doubted you, I must confess
But retrospect provides clearer sight
And I write this poem now in hopes that you might
Understand the tremendous influence you had
On a little boy once construed as bad
He's all grown now and successful too
And he owes so much of that to you!

Tip 71
Celebrate the Uniqueness of Your Students

> **I'm Not My Older Brother**
>
> *I'm not my older brother, so please do not compare*
> *To treat me as another would surely be unfair*
> *He has ways of doing things – ways that are his own*
> *He's okay, but there's no way that I'll become his clone*
> *I'm not my older brother, and I do not wish to be*
> *I'm happy to be who I am, and that is simply me.*

Said a mother of her identical twins, "They grew up at the same time in the same home with the same parents, yet they are polar opposites! Go figure." Every child is his own person with unique talents, skills, strengths, and dreams. Remember this in the classroom. **Don't ever compare students to their siblings or to other students. Rather, find the unique aspects of each student and celebrate those qualities.** I am not, of course, referring to a student's unique quality of being the most disruptive person in the classroom. Not exactly a cause for celebration. Find the strengths and talents in each student, and nurture those qualities.

A student once told me, "The thing I like best about Mr. C is that he doesn't compare me to my brothers. I'm the youngest of six boys, and we've all gone to this same school. So every year, I'm known by most of my teachers as the last of the Patterson boys. We all look alike, so they expect that we all ARE alike, and we're not. I like my brothers all right, but I don't want to walk in their footsteps. I've got my own path mapped out. Anyway, Mr. C never even mentions my brothers, and he's taught them all. He just acts as if I'm a regular guy, my own person."

Remember that each student is a unique individual, his own person. Treat him that way. Celebrate who he is rather than pushing him to be someone he's not.

To put it in its simplest terms: *I am me. I am not you. If you should think that I am you, please see me.*

> ✔ **Ask Yourself:** Do I take the time to recognize (and celebrate) the special and unique qualities of each of my students?

Tip 72
Light a Spark in Your Students

The teacher who is attempting to teach without inspiring the pupil with a desire to learn is hammering on cold iron.

—Horace Mann

What really matters is not so much what students walk away with in their *hands*, but rather how many sparks are ignited in their *hearts*. It is the TEACHER who is the key to the success of the students in the classroom. The TEACHER, not the CONTENT, determines whether students walk away *ignited* or *extinguished*. A great teacher can take *any* content and make it come to life.

I recently spoke with a seventh-grade student who had been retained three times. The student readily told me that he had never liked school because he just wasn't any good at it – that was, he said, until he encountered Mrs. Thomas, his seventh-grade teacher. From the beginning of the school year, he felt inspired. He felt successful. He could hardly believe the feeling, as it was one he had never experienced in school. His grades soared, and he soon caught up with his classmates – so much so that the school decided to move him on to the ninth grade. The following is a quote from this student: "Being in Mrs. Thomas' class was like a dream come true. She made learning fun, and she found some talents in me that no one else had ever noticed. Had I had Mrs. Thomas years ago, I would probably be in the right grade today. I'm not a failure. I guess I just needed to be inspired."

Would that we could all be Mrs. Thomases! And we can be. Be enthusiastic, and teach like a coach in a huddle motivating your players to want to win the game. Light a spark in all of your students. Set them aglow with a desire to work harder, to search for answers, to acquire deeper understandings, to love learning, and to be better people. If you can do that, then you have done your job well.

> ✔ **Ask Yourself:** What do I do, on a daily basis, to motivate and inspire my students? Do I realize that before I can light a spark in my students, I have to be on fire first?

Tip 73
Smile

A smile is a curve that sets everything straight.
—Phyllis Diller

"Don't smile until Christmas!" Have you heard it? How about this one: "Be mean until Halloween!" Sadly, there are a few veteran teachers who can't wait to share this *wisdom* with new teachers. This is anything but wisdom, and it is BAD advice. FACT: **Children need *happy* adults in their lives.** FACT: **A smile is the fastest way to a student's heart.**

Imagine sitting in a classroom all day where the teacher never smiles. Imagine refraining from smiling for even a day, much less until Christmas! Students need to see their teachers smiling – often! The most effective teachers smile most of the time, and sometimes it's fake! They do not, of course, smile at a student who is misbehaving. But the fact that they smile most of the time markedly decreases the times that students are misbehaving.

I tried an experiment with a new teacher. She was experiencing difficulties with student behavior. Upon observing her, I noticed that she never smiled one time throughout the lesson. She actually appeared angry. So we agreed that for one day she would teach with a pleasant demeanor and smile as often as possible. I gave her my phone number and asked her to call me the following night to let me know the results. The phone rang, and since smiles can literally be heard over the phone, I knew the experiment had worked. "They were so much better behaved today," she said. "And they even asked me what I was so happy about, which told me that I really needed to smile more."

Will smiling solve ALL behavior problems? No. Will it help to dramatically improve behavior in your classroom? Absolutely. And the best part is that it's free and takes no extra planning!

> ✔ **Ask Yourself:** Is my smiling face the first thing students see when they enter my classroom? Is it the last thing they see when they leave?

Tip 74
Give Your Students More Credit Than They Deserve

Aerodynamically, the bumblebee shouldn't be able to fly, but the bumblebee doesn't know it, so it goes on flying anyway.

—Mary Kay Ash

I sat at a teacher's desk one day during an observation. There, written on a note taped to her desk was the following: "My students might not be as good as I lead them to believe they are, but they'll try harder because of it." I couldn't wait to talk to her about this. When I asked her about it, she smiled and said, "That's my philosophy. I believe in giving my students just a little more credit than they deserve, and they always rise to the occasion. If they don't know they can't do something, then their chances of doing it are increased. I believe in helping students to believe in themselves, because once they believe in themselves, they're unstoppable!"

This teacher hit the nail on the head! Tell your students that they're a little better than they are, and they'll become a little better than they are. The key here is "a little." You do not want to tell a student who struggles to write a complete sentence that he is a brilliant writer. What you might do instead is give him something simple to write and then praise him when he succeeds, telling him you spot potential in his writing. Likewise, you won't want to tell a student with behavior issues that his behavior is stellar when it is clearly not. But do notice when he is behaving well and say something like, "I noticed that you worked quietly for 10 minutes. Have you noticed that your behavior is really improving? You should be proud of that." When giving students a little more credit than they might deserve, use discretion and a little common sense. There are lots of young bumblebees learning to fly in your classroom. Don't tell them they can't. Let them fly!

> ✔ **Ask Yourself:** If I give a student just a little more credit than he or she deserves, what do I stand to lose? What do both the student and I stand to gain?

Tip 75
Make Every Student Your "Favorite"

Who's My Teacher's Favorite?

Who's my teacher's favorite? I'm fairly sure it's me.
What? You think it's you instead? That simply cannot be.
Of course, now that you mention it, she treats us both the same.
She smiles at me, she smiles at you; she calls us both by name;
She helps me when I'm struggling; she does the same with you;
She helps us to be better at whatever we're trying to do;
With any classroom rules she has, she makes us both comply;
And when we feel like giving up, she encourages us to try.
So who's her favorite student, then? Neither of us can deny
That unmistakably, unequivocally, it seems to be a tie!

I often tell teachers that if I were to walk into their classrooms and ask the students who their teacher's favorite student is, all hands should go up. If a few hands remain down, I can practically guarantee that those are the students causing problems. If many hands remain down, there are widespread problems both in teaching, learning, and classroom management.

Students who do not feel that you care are the ones most likely to seek your attention in inappropriate ways or to disengage completely. The good news is that the opposite is also true. Once a student of any age level is convinced that you care about him, he will do almost anything to please you. He will act respectfully, do his work, behave appropriately, and even turn in homework! It's quite simple: Students want to feel successful, appreciated, and respected. And though the task is no small one, you should make it a priority to make each student feel that he or she is your "secret favorite." You can accomplish this by taking a personal interest in every student, making sure that each is experiencing success, and doing all the little things that tell them you care. It does not require that you let students off the hook for inappropriate behavior, of course. It simply means you hold them all accountable, you treat them all with respect, and you demonstrate that you love teaching them and care about each of them. Show me a competent teacher who treats all students as "favorites" and I'll show you a classroom with fewer behavior problems and higher levels of student achievement than a teacher of equal capability who does not treat students as favorites. In the words of Abraham Lincoln, *If you would win a man to your cause, first convince him that you are his sincere friend.*

✔ **Ask Yourself:** Do I treat all of my students as favorites, or are there a few who may question my lack of favoritism toward them? If so, what simple steps could I take to turn that around?

Tip 76
Help Any Student Succeed

When you tell a student he can do it,
And you show him how and see him through it,
Usually he'll do it and he'll succeed.
Success – it breeds success indeed!

Nathan was 15 years old and in the seventh grade. On the day he arrived, he announced to me that he was there only because he had been expelled from his previous school and that he had no intention of learning anything. He was simply biding his time until he could quit school. I knew I had to do something to make him successful, and the sooner the better! "By the way," he added, "you have a nice car." Bingo! He liked cars. He already knew which teacher drove what car. I began to allow him to teach me everything he knew about cars. In class, I used every opportunity to relate what I taught him to cars and engines. We started at his level, which was quite low, and he steadily improved. (See Tip 32 for more on teaching students at their level.) As often as possible, we read and wrote about cars. Soon he was telling ME how a particular skill reminded him of something to do with cars, engines, motorcycles, etc. He was experiencing success in school, possibly for the first time in his life. The rest of the story is that not only did he remain in school, but he went on to receive a high school diploma. No small feat for Nathan! Some years later, I was filling my gas tank at a local convenience store when I heard a deep voice say, "How about a hug?" It was Nathan. He was now a successful auto mechanic!

It is true that nothing breeds success like success. However, many students do not experience much success in school. This does not have to be the case. One of our main jobs, as teachers, is to ensure that every student succeeds. In some way, every student is Nathan. And every time he experiences the tiniest taste of success, he'll be hungry for more. Success is a process, not an overnight accomplishment. So be patient – both with yourself and with your students – and set them up for success, one bite at a time.

> ✔ **Ask Yourself:** Who, of all of my students, is experiencing the least amount of success right now? Once you determine that, work on helping that student to begin experiencing small successes. Prepare to be amazed!

Tip 77
Provide Positive Feedback

I can live for two months on a good compliment.
—Mark Twain

Research has concluded, time and again, that **it takes several positive comments to neutralize one negative comment in the brain.** However, in the typical school, negative comments far outweigh positive ones. We are all aware of the fact that positive environments are far more conducive to student cooperation and achievement than are negative environments. But research has also shown that in most schools the negative comments far outweigh the negative ones. Many classrooms often resonate with the sounds of "Don't do that," "Stop it," "Be quiet," "Pay attention," "Sit up straight," "Go to the office," etc.

In an attempt to see if it was possible to turn this situation around, I conducted an experiment. The experiment I'm about to share with you has produced amazingly positive results in every one of the 20-plus schools in which I've attempted it thus far. Here's how it works. I conduct a brief faculty in-service, sharing the information I have just shared with you regarding *positive* and *negative* comments in schools and classrooms. Then I ask the faculty for permission to conduct an experiment with them, expressing my expectations that they will defy the research. They always agree to the experiment. I tell them I will visit their classrooms and will simply be keeping a tally of positives and negatives. I will give credit for smiles, praise, constructive feedback to students, positive sayings on the walls, any type of positive comment made to students, etc. One stipulation is that students cannot be made aware of what is going on. I also tell them the date that I will be conducting the experiment, and it never fails: one or two teachers approach me afterwards and say, "You shouldn't have told everyone which day you were coming. Some of the teachers are negative, and they'll just fake being positive on the day that you're here." I always thank them for their concern and assure them that all will be fine. You see, I am intentionally setting them up for success, but they don't yet realize that.

On the day of the experiment, it is typical to identify a ratio of anywhere from 25–50 positive comments to every one negative. It is also very typical that on that day, student office referrals drop drastically. It's amazing! Teachers are smiling, students are smiling, and learning is evident. I then compile the results and return to speak to the faculty. I begin by congratulating them on their positive school environment. I provide nothing but positive feedback, and they beam with pride. They are always amazed at how well behaved the students were, especially since the students were not even aware of the experiment. And then the real lesson: I share with them the fact that several of them seemed concerned that my announcing the date of the experiment would sway the results of the experiment. Then I say, "I have just taught you a very powerful lesson about teaching. I set you up for success. I told you the date of the experiment, knowing that you would make a special effort to be positive. You see, I didn't want to *catch* you doing something negative. Had I done that with a *surprise attack* experiment, the results may not have been quite as positive. Then, had I provided negative feedback, insisting that you change your attitudes, you would have become defensive and resentful. Instead, I set you up for success so that I could provide you with some useful, positive feedback. I simply wanted to prove to you that being positive makes a BIG difference. And remember, the only thing that was different was *your* attitude, *your* approach. The students had no idea what was going on, but they responded favorably to the positive environments in your classrooms."

I encourage them to set their students up for success by maintaining a positive attitude, providing positive feedback, and expressing their belief in each student's abilities.

Oh, and something else that never fails. The assistant principals (who usually handle the discipline referrals) always ask me to come back the next day, and the next day, and the next!

> Express belief and you'll eventually SEE it.
> Tell me I AM and then watch me BE it!

✔ **Ask Yourself:** Am I aware of whether my positive comments far outweigh my negative ones in my classroom each day?

Tip 78
Use Clever Psychology

A Very Clever Teacher

We had to draw a picture one day, but I couldn't decide what to draw,
So I decided to leave my paper blank, and my teacher looked at it in awe.
"What a beautiful fluffy white cloud!" she said, "May I hang it on the wall?"
And I realized that she did not notice that I had drawn nothing at all.
Then she proudly hung for all to see the work I had not done,
But with her permission I took it home and I added the sky and the sun.
And now that I think about it, I wonder if she really knew
That my drawing was not of a cloud at all; it was work that I did not do.
I thought that I had tricked her, but maybe it was she
Who used a clever way to get me to draw a picture for all to see.

How many teachers truly use the kind of psychology that the teacher in the above poem uses? Many do, but many others do not. The general rule is: The teacher gives an assignment, the child turns in a blank paper, and the student gets an F. Now I'm not suggesting that you allow students to turn in blank papers. Rather, I'm saying that **with the right psychology, you can get a student to do just about anything.**

Liz Yates, one of the most positive teachers I have ever had the privilege of knowing, went into a classroom to observe a new teacher. The teacher was having problems with a particular student and was willing to try anything. Liz spotted the student immediately. She was a tall, over-aged student, and she had a way of making her presence known, to put it mildly. She was out of her seat, walking around, blurting out answers, picking on other students, etc. Following the observation, Liz asked the teacher for permission to speak with this student. Liz called the student out of the room, and the student followed, surmising that she was in trouble. Liz introduced herself and said, "I'm Mrs. Yates, and I work for the school board. I couldn't help noticing some things about your behavior." Now the student really assumed that she was in trouble! Liz went on to say, "I noticed that you have a way of standing out in a crowd. You've got some real leadership potential!" The student, dumbfounded, listened attentively. "I also noticed," said Liz, "that you're very knowledgeable." (You see, she had noted that even though the student was blurting out answers, the answers were correct!) "Have you ever thought about being a teacher when you grow up?" asked Liz. "You know, if you could learn to temper your behavior a little, I think that both you and others would really benefit from your skills and abilities. You've got some real possibilities." The student thanked Liz and went back into the classroom. Liz told the teacher about how she had handled the situation, and the teacher decided to give that same psychology a try. Months later, Liz went back into that classroom. The student ran up to Liz, called her by name, hugged her, and said, "I've decided to be a teacher, and I've really been practicing hard!" The teacher told Liz that the child had become a model student. "She participates in class, she behaves very well, she's working on managing her tendency to express her opinions inappropriately, and she now stays in at recess to tutor the same students she used to tease. I can't believe the difference, and I'm amazed at what a little psychology can accomplish!" said the teacher.

Using clever psychology can be both fascinating and fun. Of course, **the right psychology requires the right attitude.** Any effective teacher will tell you that *attitude* will make or break you in the classroom. So adopt the attitude of helping students to help themselves. Be resolved to turn potentially negative situations into positive ones. Model an attitude of optimism. Convince students that you believe in them – especially when they are having trouble believing in themselves.

✔ **Ask Yourself:** Do I have any students who occasionally act out or refuse to do work? Is my current approach working? If not, try a little clever psychology. You have nothing to lose, and your students have everything to gain.

Tip 79
Focus on the Positives in Your Classroom

Keep your face to the sunshine and you cannot see the shadows.
–Helen Keller

I once watched a speaker make a profound statement to his audience through the use of an activity. He had the audience look around the room. They had 30 seconds to locate and memorize everything they saw that was yellow. The activity began, and everyone scanned the room for yellow objects. After 30 seconds, he had them close their eyes. He then said, "Now make a mental list of everything in this room that is black." The participants, stunned, could not remember one thing that was black. (Their eyes were still closed.) He then had them open their eyes and look around. They were amazed that there were many more black objects in the room than yellow. However, since they had focused on yellow, that's all they had seen. Point? "Keep your face to the sunshine (yellow) and you cannot see the shadows (black)." The speaker made the profound point that life is what we focus on. In our classrooms, at any given time, there are negatives (black) and there are positives (yellow). If we look hard enough, we will find something negative, if that's where we place our focus. The good news is that the same holds true for the positives in our classrooms. It can be easy, at times, to get frustrated and focus on all that's wrong. It may sound like this: "Don't do that." "Sit down." "Sit up straight." "Stop it." "Pay attention!" "Get quiet." "Don't make me send you to the principal." Interestingly, students do tend to live up to the expectations of their teachers, so inappropriate behaviors are actually being encouraged in this type of classroom. Conversely, these are phrases you will hear often in the classroom of someone focusing on positives: "Thank you for raising your hand." "Great job!" "I appreciate your attentiveness to this important task." "I'm so proud of you." Once again, students tend to meet our expectations, so in this case, positive behaviors are being encouraged. This is not to suggest that nothing negative ever happens in the classroom of a positive teacher. However, these incidences are rare and are dealt with in a respectful manner. Effective teachers know that focusing on positive behaviors will foster positive behaviors.

✔ **Ask Yourself:** Do I tend to focus on the sunshine or the shadows?

Tip 80
Display Student Work

When I do work and you display it,
it says you're proud and you want to convey it!

During a visit to a ninth-grade science class, I immediately noticed that the classroom walls consisted of lots of student work and pictures of students working. The teacher said to the students, "Tell Ms. Breaux about what we've been learning." They began pointing to their projects around the room and their work samples on the walls. After I remarked about one particular project, a student quickly led me to pictures taken while the students were completing the project – a photographic display of every step of the process. The students wanted to show me everything and tell me about all they had been doing. One of the students wanted to take a photograph of them explaining their work to me. The teacher readily picked up his camera and snapped a few shots while the students continued to speak of their accomplishments. Then one student said, "Oh, let me show a picture of the experiment that didn't work." He quickly led me to a photograph, and beneath it was a poster titled, "What We Learned from This Mistake."

When I was speaking with the teacher afterwards, he told me that the classroom belonged to everyone, so he believed in giving everyone equal ownership. He said, "Everyone has work displayed. That's because every student experiences success in my class. But notice that there are no graded assignments on the walls. If I did that, only the brightest students would have their work displayed. I want everyone's work up there, and they all want their work up there, too. For some, it's the first time they've ever had their work showcased. I've also noticed that the more pictures I take, the harder they work. They love to see pictures of themselves working."

Displaying student work works! And it's free. Make the classroom theirs, and allow your students to showcase their talents.

> ✔ **Ask Yourself:** How much student work is displayed in my classroom right now? Can I find a few spots on the wall to add some more? And can I snap a few pictures of students working and post them both in the classroom and on our online class page so parents can see it too?

Tip 81
Have Positive Expectations for ALL Students

Treat people as if they were what they ought to be, and you'll help them to become what they are capable of becoming.

—Johann Wolfgang von Goethe

Years back, I had an experience I will never forget. It was the week before school began, and I attended a meeting for parents and teachers. The parents of Raneesha said to me, "We're apologizing in advance for Raneesha's attitude." "What do you mean?" I asked. I had not even met Raneesha yet. "Well, she's got a real attitude problem. Any teacher who's ever taught her can tell you that, and we see it at home every day. We tell her that her attitude is bad, but that doesn't change her. Just let us know when she gets out of line, and we'll deal with her." Knowing that I needed to address that situation from day one, I decided that I would find any opportunity to capitalize on any hint of a positive attitude I could manage to find in Raneesha. I was a little apprehensive about meeting her, yet I was determined to have high expectations. On the first day of school, Raneesha walked into my class. I introduced myself, and she reluctantly shook my hand. I then said, "You look like someone I can trust. Would you please bring this very important envelope to the secretary for me?" (The envelope was empty, and the secretary already knew to expect it.) "Yes," answered Raneesha, with a hint of a smile on her face. "Thank you so much," I responded. "I love your attitude!" I said. From that moment on, Raneesha displayed a model attitude in my class. But I never let up on mentioning her positive attitude to her as often as possible. Every chance I got, I said, "I love your attitude!" About six weeks later, Raneesha stayed after class one day to hand me a letter from her parents. "What's this?" I asked. "It's a letter from my parents. They wanted to tell you that my attitude has improved a lot at home, and they want to thank you for helping me with that." Acting totally oblivious to her past history, I said, "What do you mean by improved? How could your attitude possibly improve? You've got one of the best attitudes I've ever seen in a seventh grader." Raneesha went on to explain to me what I already knew – the fact that her attitude had previously left a lot to be desired, both at home and at school. "So why the sudden change?" I asked. "Well, I thought about that a lot," said Raneesha. "Remember on the first day of school when you told me I had a good attitude? I guess I figured you didn't know any better and that maybe I did have a good attitude hidden inside of me somewhere. You were the first person that ever told me anything positive about my attitude. It was like you just expected me to have a good attitude, so I did."

This is just one small, yet profound example of how students will live up to your expectations. If you treat students as if you expect them to be successful, whether it is in their studies or in their dealings with others, and if you start with very small successes and capitalize on those successes as opposed to reinforcing negative expectations, then they will become what they are capable of becoming! **Just as we tend to get out of life what we expect out of life, we tend to get out of our students what we expect out of our students.**

> ✔ **Ask Yourself:** Do I treat EVERY student as if he or she is capable of succeeding?

Tip 82
Get to Know Your Students

I Wish My Teacher Knew Me

I wish my teacher knew me. Instead, she looks right through me.
But if she stopped and looked inside, she'd see the good I try to hide.
And when she did, she'd be surprised by all she never realized.
And she wouldn't misconstrue me, if only my teacher knew me.

A teacher was having problems with a student, and she called for my assistance. She described the problem student – I will call him T.J. – as lazy, tuned-out, uncaring, unfeeling, and disrespectful. He rarely did his work in class and he never did homework. In fact, she had been sending him to the principal, to no avail. "What do you know about his home life?" I asked. "I don't have time to delve into these students' home lives," she responded. "I barely have time to get my work done at school. Besides, I've got enough of my own problems at home." As it turned out, T.J.'s parents were suspected drug dealers. T.J. was living in a small apartment with aunts, uncles, cousins, siblings, and questionable others. T.J.'s bed at night consisted of a board placed over the bathtub! And yet here was a teacher sending him to the principal for not turning in homework. When I told the teacher what I had learned about T.J.'s home life, she was shocked. And she realized that maybe it was with good reason that T.J. was not a model student. "Wow," she said, "and I thought I had problems."

You see, every student has a story. Some stories are good ones and some are tragic. Regardless, it is vital that we attempt to learn something personal (without prying, of course) about each student. Get to know all you can about your students – become interested in their dreams, their cultural differences, their varied interests, and their stories. Once we know them as "real people," it makes it easier for us to understand them and to help them. And though we cannot change our students' home lives, we can most certainly help them to have positive, successful experiences in school. T.J. deserved to have a teacher who took an interest in him, who got to know him, and who cared about him as a person. No, you cannot know everything there is to know about every student, but you can know *something*.

✔ **Ask Yourself:** Are there any of my students I don't know much about yet? If so, what can I do, today, to change that?

Tip 83
Encourage Improvement, Not Perfection

During his career, the great Babe Ruth hit 714 homeruns.
He also struck out 1330 times!

In the sport of baseball, many, many of the "greats" have made it into the Hall of Fame with a .300 lifetime batting average or less. That means that they *failed* 70% of the time at bat! Yet they are considered extremely successful – the best of the best. In school, however, you have to succeed at least 70% of the time in order to barely get by with a passing grade. Try to imagine ANY area of your life where you are successful for more than 70% of the time. I'll bet you'll have a difficult time doing that. In football, almost every play is technically designed to score points. However, almost every play does NOT score points. But that doesn't stop the coach from attempting to have his team score points on the next play. Find a parent who succeeds 70% of the time with everything he tries to teach his child. That parent does not exist. Better yet, find a stockbroker who succeeds with 70% of all of his stock trades. If you do, call me. I'll invest!

The point is that we often label students as failures because we are making the mistake of encouraging perfection in all of them. This is the way we were *trained* to think in school. Admit it – if you took a test with 100 questions and received a grade of 95%, you would immediately look for the five that you missed as opposed to the 95 that you got right! And many of you would be upset with anything less than 100%. In a conversation with a teacher, I learned that she had many students who were experiencing what she called "no success at all." In looking more closely at the situation, I learned that these students were struggling with content that was way above their levels. Amazingly, they were managing to score 50% or better on her tests. I saw some real potential here, and I shared my observations with this teacher. I said, "I'm going to speak to you in Chinese and I'm going to teach you in Chinese and then I'll test you in Chinese. What do you think you'll score?" "Well, I don't know how to speak Chinese, so I'll score a zero," she said. (I don't speak Chinese either, by the way, but I was just trying to make a point.) "Don't you think you could at least get half of all the answers correct?" I asked. "No way," she said. "Well, what you're trying to teach these particular struggling students is material that's far above their levels of understanding. It's almost as if you were speaking and teaching and testing in a language that is foreign to them. Yet they're getting at least half of it correct. Wow! What potential!" I exclaimed. "I never thought of it that way," said the teacher. "I think I see where you're going with this. I need to speak in 'their' language, at 'their' levels." "Absolutely," I answered. "And then move them forward from there. You'll be amazed at their progress, based on their potential and their obvious tendencies to be overachievers!" I added.

The teacher began, the very next day, to teach these students from their current levels of understanding. Then, she agreed that she would focus only on improvement, not perfection. Within a few weeks, these students had made enormous strides. By the end of the semester, each of them was able to pass the course. No, they did not make straight As, but they did pass. And they were experiencing success unlike they had ever before experienced.

In the classroom, we should teach students that improvement is what matters. Perfection is not only impossible, but striving for it will give you ulcers and will drive the people around you out of their minds! Success is attainable for anyone, one step at a time. Homeruns are great, but strikeouts are opportunities to improve your skills. An enthusiastic "swing and a miss" has led many people to greatness.

> ✔ **Ask Yourself:** Do I express, in no uncertain terms, that I only ask for improvement – not perfection – from my students? And do I show them, daily, how to take small steps in order to experience that improvement?

Tip 84
Avoid Sarcasm

The inner landscape of many children is full of mines ready to explode upon careless contact. Any insulting remark can set off an explosion.

—*Haim Ginott*

"What time is it?" asked a student. "I'll tell you what time it is. It's time for you to be quiet," answered the teacher in a less than pleasant tone. Having been seated in the classroom for the past 15 or so minutes, I knew that this student had been busily and quietly at work. "Why the sarcasm?" I wondered. A few minutes later, most of the students had finished their assignments. Naturally, some of them began whispering to one another. "Excuse me!" barked the teacher, "You're supposed to be working, not talking." "We're finished," said some of the students. "Well, I had better not find any mistakes on your papers," answered the teacher. "I can't figure out problem number 4," said another student. "Well, maybe if the rest of your classmates would be engaging their brains instead of their mouths, you might be able to concentrate better," huffed the teacher. By this point, almost everyone was talking. The teacher grew angrier and became more sarcastic, which finally led to a hostile confrontation with a student. "Open your mouth one more time, and you're going straight to the office," yelled the teacher. "I'm not going to the office unless everyone else goes," said the student, "because they're all talking, too!"

This situation went from bad to worse. And this teacher felt victimized by her students. In actuality, her negative tone and sarcastic words were provoking the same behaviors in her students – not to mention the fact that there was too much time where students had nothing to do. Her lack of management led to talking, which made her angry and evoked sarcasm. Regardless, there is simply no place for sarcasm in the classroom. **Sarcasm accomplishes nothing positive, it's completely unprofessional, and it shows a lack of control on the part of the teacher.** Most students already have to deal with enough cynicism in their lives. As teachers, we're supposed to lift them, build their self-esteem, encourage their endeavors, and model the behaviors we hope they emulate. Using sarcasm will help accomplish none of these behaviors. **What time is it? It's time for all of us to take a good look at our behaviors with students and refrain from using any kind of comments that may even *hint* of sarcasm.**

> ✔ **Ask Yourself:** When is it appropriate to use sarcasm with a student? The answer, of course, is never. You may be tempted to, but save that sarcasm for the adults in your life. (Kidding . . . maybe. . . .)

Tip 85

Be "Human" to Your Students

I Never Thought of Her That Way

I saw my teacher shopping in the grocery store today.
What? She shops for groceries? I never thought of her that way.
And I looked inside her basket – and her food was normal too.
She was pushing her basket and walking around like normal people do.
I thought she lived in the classroom – just stayed there night and day
But it appears she may be normal – I never thought of her that way!

If you have ever encountered one of your students in the grocery store or at a social function, then you will know that the above poem is true. It's almost as though you're a celebrity when you're recognized by your students outside of school. "Wow! She actually shops for groceries!" Students don't automatically see you as *human*. They see you as their teacher, period. And though there is a fine line that you do not want to cross, you do want to become as human as possible to your students. So what's the fine line? The fine line is crossed when you provide too much information. Your students don't need to know about your personal problems. They don't need to know about your date last night. They don't need to know about all of your after-school activities or all of the details of your at-home life. But they can know about some.

In their book, *The First Days of School*, Harry and Rosemary Wong encourage teachers to create a personality bulletin board. It simply requires making a bulletin board about yourself. Items on the bulletin board may include your hobbies, your interests, pictures of you when you were in school, your school report cards (if you dare!), your family's pictures, awards you have received, your diplomas, etc. It's such a simple idea, and it truly makes a big difference in becoming *human* to your students. Give it a try. Be human to your students, and they will respect you more. Students need to know that you are a living, breathing individual who possibly made less-than-perfect grades when you were in school, too!

> ✔ **Ask Yourself:** Do my students know a little about who I am as a person? Do they see me as a real human being or as just a teacher who probably lives in the classroom?

Wong, H.K. and Wong, R.T. (2009). *The First Days of School: How to Be an Effective Teacher.* Mountain View, CA: Harry K. Wong Publications.

Tip 86
Refer to Yourself in the First Person

1st person: *person speaking (I, me, my, mine, etc.)*
2nd person: *person spoken to (you, your, yours, etc.)*
3rd person: *person spoken of (she, he, it, they, etc.).*

To emphasize the point I'm trying to make, I'm going to speak to you in the third person. Imagine that you are in the room with me, and I begin speaking to you in this way: "Ms. Breaux is very glad that you're reading Ms. Breaux's book. She is hoping that it will help you improve your teaching. She really wants you to pay special attention to what is meant by speaking in the first person."

Wouldn't that seem strange that I'm referring to myself almost as if I'm not there or as if I'm speaking of someone else? What comes naturally is to say, "I'm very glad that you're reading my book. I'm hoping that it will help you improving your teaching. I really want you to pay special attention to what is meant by speaking in the first person."

So why is it that some teachers speak to their students using the third person when speaking of themselves? It sounds like this: "Good morning, students. Ms. Breaux wants you to take out your English books. Ms. Breaux will be showing you how to . . . . " I know you'll recognize it, because it's definitely a *teacher* thing. I have yet to hear anyone in any other profession refer to themselves in the third person. What teachers don't realize is that it sounds condescending and it creates a "distance" or "barrier" between them and their students when they say, "Ms. Breaux is very proud of you," or, "Ms. Breaux doesn't like the way you're behaving." Many teachers do this without thinking about it. It's a learned habit. And though I have witnessed this behavior at all grade levels, I have definitely noticed it most in the elementary grades. Ms. Breaux is now finished making Ms. Breaux's point here.

> ✔ **Ask Yourself:** Do I ever call myself by my own name when speaking to my students? If so, you may want to rethink it. Speaking in the first person is modeling *natural* speech, and it also makes your conversations with others more personal.

Tip 87
Remember That Little Things Make a Big Difference

It has long been an axiom of mine that the little things are infinitely the most important.

—*Sherlock Holmes*

FACT: The little things in life make the biggest difference. A simple pat on the back or a smile might be just what someone needs to brighten up his day. Sadly, for some students, your smile is the only smile they may receive that day. In the classroom, little things make a huge difference to your students. And, by the way, they cost nothing. Here is a list of a few *little things* you can do that will make a *big difference* to your students:

- Acknowledge student birthdays.
- Greet each student with a smile as he or she enters your classroom, and send them off with a smile when they leave.
- Compliment students on jobs well done.
- Make a positive phone call (or send a note, text, or e-mail) to a parent regarding something his child has accomplished in class.
- Write encouraging comments on student work.
- Visit a sick student in the hospital, or at least make a phone call.
- Write a thank-you note to a student who has given you a gift.
- Notice haircuts.
- Give a thumbs up to a student for a job well done.
- Notice and acknowledge little kindnesses which students show to others.
- Attend school functions to show support.
- Ask students about their hobbies and interests.
- Notice and encourage even the smallest of student successes.

Although this list is by no means all-inclusive, it reminds us of the little things that we sometimes overlook or underestimate.

> ✔ **Ask Yourself**: Do I realize what a BIG difference it makes when I take the time to show lots of little kindnesses to my students?

Tip 88
Dignify Incorrect Responses

FACT: If you maintain a student's dignity, you will see lasting results.
If you take away a student's dignity, you may face lasting revenge.

In Tip 18, we discussed the importance of avoiding power struggles with students. It has been my observation that teachers often engage in power struggles with students when students either do not know the answer to a question or, better yet, when they give a *ridiculous* answer intentionally. Here's an actual classroom example:

The class was discussing United States presidents. The teacher asked, "Who was our first president?" One student in the back of the room raised his hand and then gave the name of a famous talk-show host. The students, of course, found this quite amusing. The teacher now had a choice – she could enter into a power struggle and show frustration and aggravation, or she could take all energy away from the student, discreetly discouraging that type of answer, maintaining her composure, and still managing to maintain the student's dignity. Had she chosen to play, she would have probably said the following, in a tone of frustration and aggravation: "Very funny. Are you finished with your comedy routine? Now if you can't give serious answers, don't give any at all." This, of course, would have added more fuel to the fire, increasing the likelihood of the same behavior in the future. However, this teacher amazed me, as she looked at the student reassuringly and said, "I know exactly what you're thinking. You're thinking of a male, and both the talk-show host you mentioned and the first president are males, and you're thinking of a famous person, and both of these men are famous. Good thinking. Now can someone tell me the name of the first president?" Another student answered correctly, and the student with the sarcastic answer was completely defused. He looked a little shocked, thinking that his answer was not so far off after all, as his teacher had just given him some credit. For the rest of the discussion he remained actively involved, and on two occasions he volunteered correct answers.

Following the lesson, I commended the teacher on the way she had handled that situation. She said, "Oh, well, he's a new student, and he's just trying to fit in. So I'm going to do my best to see that he does fit in, but in a positive way. Besides that, I never give any energy to those kinds of things. I've got bigger fish to fry!"

On the very same day, I was observing in another classroom where one of the students gave an incorrect answer, but not an intentionally incorrect answer. This teacher responded by saying, "We've been talking about this for a week now. Where have you been?" I was appalled, but more important was the fact that this poor student was embarrassed. Not surprisingly, this student did absolutely nothing for the rest of the class period. She shut down completely and was reprimanded once again by the teacher – this time for being inattentive.

When students shut down, we lose them. And if we are the cause of that *shutting down*, then we are facing inevitable discipline problems atop the inevitable academic problems. Students may give incorrect answers, but at least they're participating! And those incorrect answers assist us in monitoring their understanding or lack of understanding of a concept. And, by the way, if students are giving all correct answers, you should be moving on to things they *don't* know! The secret is to dignify incorrect responses, whether those answers are intentional or not.

Here's a quick trick for you. If you feel as though you're not quick enough on your feet to think of how to respond when a student gives an incorrect answer, whether intentional or not, you can always smile and say, "I know exactly what you're thinking," and move on. You dignified the answer without giving the kind of attention that might embarrass a student who was giving his best answer or spur the student who was simply trying to push your buttons to be even more "creative" next time.

✔ **Ask Yourself:** When students give incorrect answers unintentionally, how do I react? Do I maintain their dignity? When students give incorrect answers on purpose, how do I react? Do I avoid fueling the flame and simply defuse the situation, or do I let them know I'm aggravated?

Tip 89
Avoid Nagging

You nag nag nag nag
And I gag gag gag gag
What a drag drag drag drag
When you nag nag nag nag.

The best way to describe *nagging* is by defining it in teacher terms. Nagging means taking way too long to make a point that could have been stated in a few words. Here's an example:

A student has had difficulty turning in homework assignments. One day, she brings in an assignment on time. A "nagging" teacher says, "Mary, why can't you bring in your assignments on time every day? If you can do it once, you can do it again. Doesn't it feel good to have your assignment turned in on time? If you would only do this every time, I wouldn't have to punish you and constantly be on your back about it. Then we'd both be happier. I'm hoping you've learned a lesson from this. Have you?"

Do you notice how the teacher goes on and on and on? That's nagging. Now let's look at the same situation from a non-nagging standpoint: *"Great, Mary. Thanks for bringing your assignment in on time. I'm so proud of you."* This scenario is an example of encouraging as opposed to nagging the student. Students respond much better to encouragement than they do to nagging. (So do adults!) Now, in order not to sound as if I'm nagging you about nagging, I'll end this section, since I've made my point!

> ✔ **Ask Yourself:** Do I make every effort to make my points with students succinctly and avoid nagging at all costs?

Tip 90
Laugh with Your Students

Laughing, laughing, wonderful laughter
You laugh so hard that your stomach hurts after
Now each time you think of it, the laughter returns
And while laughing you lose sight of all your concerns
So think of it often and laugh laugh laugh
For laughter cuts most of life's troubles in half.

Many studies have been conducted on laughter and many books have been written on the subject. Basically, they all say the same thing: Laughter is the best medicine! It has been proven that laughing releases endorphins (in the brain) that boost our immune systems and make us happier. Laughing feels good. Environments where laughter abounds are happy places. Studies have also shown that children laugh a lot more each day than adults. I don't think any of us would doubt that, but maybe it helps to explain why children are happier and healthier than adults! Students love teachers who laugh with them. Yes, there are times when laughter is not appropriate. That's common sense. But when the opportunity presents itself – and it will present itself often in the classroom – have a good laugh with your students.

Regrettably, many teachers will readily admit that they don't laugh very often in the classroom. I once asked a teacher why she thought this was so, and she answered, "Because teaching is a serious business!" Needless to say, she was struggling desperately with managing student behavior. The students weren't having fun *with* the teacher, so they decided to have fun *without* her! Students want to have fun, and they will create ways to have fun if you don't provide those ways.

> ✔ **Ask Yourself:** How often do I laugh with my students? do I laugh with them every day, or have I become a little too serious? If so, start laughing and release some endorphins. Classrooms with "high endorphin levels" are classrooms with higher learning levels.

Tip 91
Be an Optimist

Is your glass half empty or half full???

In life, there are optimists and there are pessimists. You've known people on both sides. You've probably been on both sides yourself. Everyone, at some point in their lives, can be either. What's important is to live, most of the time, in the land of optimism – especially if you are teaching students! Consider the following two poems.

Oh, Woe is Me

Oh, woe is me, I am a teacher – parent, doctor, therapist, preacher,
Battling daily with the youth, whose attitudes are more than uncouth.
A disciplinarian, no stranger to force; don't talk to me after 3:30 – I'm hoarse.
One year of experience 20 times o'er; I teach each year like the year before.
My students are disrespectful and lazy, yet they look at me like I am crazy.
If it weren't for students, my life would be swell, and my job wouldn't seem like a living hell.
Speaking of which, I've gotta go. My principal's coming – gotta put on a show!

I Teach

I light a spark in a darkened soul, I warm the heart of one grown cold,
I look beyond and see within – behind the face, beneath the skin,
I quench a thirst, I soothe a pain, I provide the food that will sustain,
I touch, I love, I laugh, I cry. Whatever is needed, I supply.
Yet more than I give, I gain from each. I am most richly blessed – I teach!

✔ **Ask Yourself:** Which of the two poems best describes me?

Tip 92
Thank Your Students Often

The deepest principle of human nature is the craving to be appreciated.
—*William James*

In Tip 87, we discussed the fact that little things make a big difference to students. Saying "thank you" is one of those little things we can do. Here are some of the benefits of saying "thank you": it's free, it tells students that you care, it makes students feel appreciated and special, it models appropriate manners, it encourages students to do better and to be better, it sets a tone of encouragement in the classroom, and it promotes a positive learning environment.

I had the privilege of observing a teacher who thanks her students more often than any teacher I've ever observed. Here are some of the statements I heard during this observation:

- *"Thank you for getting to work so quickly."*
- *"Thank you for sharing that with us."*
- *"Thank you for understanding that we cannot chew gum in class." (This was said to a student who WAS chewing gum. The student immediately disposed of the gum.)*
- *"Thank you for not bringing the problems from recess into the classroom. I know it's a really difficult thing to do. If you want to discuss it, we'll do that privately. Thanks for understanding that." (This was said to a student who WAS bringing his problems from recess into the classroom. He immediately got quiet.)*
- *"Thank you for that answer."*
- *"Thank you for making that mistake. We can all learn from it."*
- *"Thank you for remembering to bring in your homework."*
- *"Thanks for your help. I appreciate you."*

Not surprisingly, this teacher had almost zero discipline problems. Is it any wonder? And yet, she taught lots of *challenging* students every year. In her classroom, however, her students were successful, they were polite, they worked diligently, and they adored her.

✔ **Ask Yourself:** How often do I say "thank you" to my students? Could I say it even more?

Motivation and Rapport: Section Highlights

- Remember that in order to motivate students, you have to be (and appear) motivated first.
- Be a "happy influence" in your students' lives by smiling often. Greet them, teach them, and leave them with a smile every day.
- Tell a student he's a little better than he is, and he just may become that good.
- Treat every student as your favorite student.
- Lead a student to a small success, and build on that success. Every small taste of it makes them hungry for the next bite.
- Ensure that your positive comments to students far outweigh your negative ones.
- Display student work and pictures all around the room – and even in the hallway.
- Treat students as if they are good and successful and they will become better and more successful. (The opposite is also true.)
- Get to know all you can about your students – become interested in their dreams, their cultural differences, their varied interests, and their stories.
- Help students aim for improvement, not perfection.
- Avoid cynicism and sarcasm. Treat all students with dignity.
- Become human to your students – possibly by displaying a teacher bulletin board telling them who you are.
- Acknowledge student birthdays, compliment them, and do all the little things that help cement positive relationships.
- Stop yourself from belaboring your point (nagging) when dealing with students.
- Make laughter a daily experience in your classroom.
- Say two simple words to students – thank you – for jobs well done.

Section Six

A Teacher's Influence

My Teacher of Many Years Ago

My teacher of many years ago influences me today.
The things that he instilled in me have never gone away.
In fact, they are a part of every fiber of my being,
The blood that courses through me and the eyes through which I'm
*   seeing,*
The love that I am giving; the decisions that I'm making,
The things that I've accomplished and the ones I'm undertaking.
For once someone influences you, he lives inside your heart,
And so of all I am today, my teacher is a part.

Tip 93
Realize That You Will Affect Lives

A child's life is like a piece of paper on which every passerby leaves a mark.
—Chinese Proverb

As teachers – as everyday, normal, run-of-the-mill individuals – we often tend to underestimate the fact that we truly do affect the lives of every student we teach. Your influence can be very powerful – hopefully in a positive sense – yet it can also be very harmful if you do not treat this *power* with the utmost reverence and respect. You see, it is often easy to say things out of frustration – things we may think nothing of, but that students will internalize and take to heart.

A teacher shared an experience with me. "I'm an accomplished musician. I teach at the university level; I perform, and I have been quite successful in my career. Isn't it sad that I cannot even balance a checkbook? And it's all because of my fifth-grade teacher." "What do you mean?" I asked. "Well," she said, "I remember it like it was yesterday. I was standing at the board, struggling to work through a math problem. The teacher was so frustrated with me, and she let the whole class know it. She told me I would never be any good at math. Guess what! I never was. It affected me so intensely that I developed a mental block when it came to math, and I've struggled with it all my life."

Ironically, she recently received a letter from one of her former music students who said, "How often we underestimate the power of words. I will never forget the five words you spoke to me which have stayed with me all my life. The words were, 'I'm so proud of you.'" So from one individual's story comes a perfect example of both the positive and the negative power of a teacher's influence. Never underestimate just how influential you really are. And know that your students will eventually leave you, but the memory of you (and your influence – positive or negative) will never leave them.

> ✔ **Ask Yourself:** Do I realize that anything I say to a student can affect who he is today and who he will eventually become? And do I realize that I will walk around in each student's memory long after he or she is gone from my classroom?

Tip 94
Remember Your Favorite Teacher

The mediocre teacher tells. The good teacher explains. The superior teacher demonstrates. The great teacher inspires.

—William Arthur Ward

Call up a mental image of your all-time favorite teacher. We all had one. Got it? You're probably already smiling at this point. Now before you read any further, make a list of several characteristics of that teacher, including what made him or her your favorite. Please don't read on until you do this.

I have conducted this activity with thousands of teachers over the years and will share some commonalities in their lists. I'll bet that you'll see more than a few similarities with your own list.

- My favorite teacher was nice.
- My favorite teacher made me feel special.
- My favorite teacher smiled a lot.
- My favorite teacher found ways to make me succeed.
- My favorite teacher made learning fun.
- My favorite teacher did not yell at me or embarrass me in front of my peers.
- My favorite teacher treated me with respect.
- My favorite teacher did not struggle with discipline problems.
- My favorite teacher inspired me.
- My favorite teacher made lessons interesting.
- My favorite teacher loved teaching.
- My favorite teacher loved children.

Did you find some similarities with your own list? Notice that nothing in that list tells about the teacher's credentials. I have yet to find someone who says, "My favorite teacher had three college degrees." And notice that nothing in that list tells of the amount of material the teacher had students memorize. And take special notice that the list tends to focus on the teacher as a person and how that teacher made students feel: special, loved, successful, inspired.

> ✔ **Ask Yourself:** Would my students list similar characteristics about me?

Tip 95
Remember Your Least Favorite Teacher

*By the nature of your position, you will influence the life of every student
you teach. Whether that influence is a positive or a negative one, it will
most certainly be a lasting one!*

In the previous tip, I had you list the characteristics of your favorite teacher.
This time we will repeat the same process, except that you will be listing the
characteristics of your least favorite teacher. Remember not to read on until
you have called up the image of this person and listed several characteristics.

Just as in the previous tip, I have conducted this activity with thousands
of teachers and have found uncanny similarities in their lists. You will likely
see more than a few similarities with your own list.

- ◆ My least favorite teacher was not a very nice person.
- ◆ My least favorite teacher rarely smiled.
- ◆ My least favorite teacher didn't care if I succeeded.
- ◆ My least favorite teacher's class was boring.
- ◆ My least favorite teacher yelled at students and humiliated them.
- ◆ My least favorite teacher treated students disrespectfully.
- ◆ My least favorite teacher had lots of discipline problems.
- ◆ My least favorite teacher did not inspire me.
- ◆ My least favorite teacher did not like teaching.
- ◆ My least favorite teacher did not like children.

Notice that the above characteristics are in direct opposition to the
characteristics in the previous tip. Also note that your feelings about your
least favorite teacher are the antithesis of your feelings about your favorite
teacher. I have often seen adults conjure up sadness and anger when
remembering their least favorite teacher. Most can remember, in the minutest
of detail, specific things that this teacher said or did to hurt or upset them.
Usually, these incidents occurred years ago, yet just thinking about their
least favorite teacher brings those unpleasant feelings back to the surface.
Also, I have yet to find anyone who says the following: "My least favorite

teacher really inspired me, but I just didn't like him." The fact is that if you can convince a student that you care, if you can inspire him, and if you can help him succeed, you will always fall into the favorite teacher category. So remember your least favorite and favorite teachers, and use their lessons to remind you of what you do and do NOT want to represent in your students' lives.

> ✔ **Ask Yourself:** Realizing that my influence will long outlive me, what kind of legacy do I want to leave?

Tip 96
Inspire for a Lifetime

If you plan for a year, plant a seed.
If for ten years, plant a tree.
If for a hundred years, teach the people.
When you sow a seed once, you will reap a single harvest.
When you teach the people, you will reap a hundred harvests.

—Kuan Chung

Students are much more in need of inspiration than they are of information. The information we provide is important, but the inspiration we provide is life-altering. An inspired individual will achieve great things. An informed individual will accomplish nothing if he lacks inspiration.

Here are three quick steps to inspiring students:

1. Be (or act) inspired yourself.
2. Express your belief in students – enthusiastically. Act as though you KNOW they will succeed and can't wait to celebrate that success.
3. Set them up for small successes. This will lead to bigger ones.

It has been said that when a butterfly just moves its wings off the California coast, it flutters the breezes that rustle the leaves on the islands of Japan. The connection is that subtle. The influence of a teacher is lifelong, and it is important that we recognize and capitalize on that fact. If you inspire one student, you affect his entire future, and you literally change the world. Through your actions as a teacher, you have the opportunity to inspire every student who ever walks through your classroom door. You really are changing this world, one student at a time. What an awesome responsibility! May you never take it lightly.

> ✔ **Ask Yourself:** Do I set as my foremost goal each day to inspire and set my students' minds afire?

Tip 97
Keep an "I Am Special" Folder

Do you ever have one of those days when you question whether you're making a difference?

Whether you are a new or a veteran teacher, it's never too late to start keeping an "I Am Special" folder. It's a very simple concept with exceptional rewards. An "I Am Special" folder is a folder in which you will keep notes from students, thank-you cards, letters or e-mails of appreciation, notes to yourself on something exciting or heartwarming that happens to you on a particular day, notes from parents, etc. (Of course, it can be a digital folder if you choose to just scan written cards, notes, etc. into it.) On those really difficult days when you are questioning whether you truly are making a difference, just take out the folder and begin to look through it. It will reaffirm the fact that you are making a difference, it will rekindle your love of children and teaching, and it will remind you that you have truly chosen the noblest of all professions!

A high school coach recently reminded me that I had given him an "I Am Special" folder when he had come through one of my new-teacher trainings a few years prior. He shared with me that he thought the idea of keeping such a folder was probably more appropriate for elementary teachers, but he decided to give it a try regardless. He told me that he began keeping newspaper clippings from games, notes from players, notes from parents, and notes he had written on occasion when he felt he had been able to light a spark in one of his players. He proudly told me that his folder had gotten so thick that he had had to start a second one!

As teachers, we are special to so many students. But sometimes we need a reminder. An "I Am Special" folder will do the trick! I still have mine, and it is one of my most valued possessions.

> ✔ **Ask Yourself:** Do I ever need a bit of inspiration to help remind me why I even chose this profession? Every teacher does. That's why every teacher should keep an "I Am Special" folder. Start yours today.

Tip 98
Teach Students That Mistakes are Wonderful Learning Opportunities

---

The Biggest Mistake

The biggest mistake that you can make is to be afraid of making a mistake.
For if you're afraid to make a mistake, no risks or chances will you take.
And if no risks or chances you take, and if you put nothing of yourself at stake
You'll walk through life asleep, not awake, and not one difference will you make!

What happened to you the first time you tried to ride a bicycle on your own? You fell off. The first time you tried to tie your own shoelaces? It didn't *quite* work out. What is typically the first word that a baby speaks? Da-da. I've checked the dictionary, and there's no such word. The baby makes a *mistake*. And what do we, as parents, do? We praise the mistake and encourage the baby. We post videos letting everyone know that our baby has spoken his first word. We even go so far as to start making the mistake ourselves, saying, "Where's da-da?" We would never dream of saying, "No, don't say that" to the baby. And we definitely would never think of labeling him a *non-talker*. This is because parents know that this *mistake* is a necessary part of learning to speak. All parents know that the *mistake* will eventually correct itself, so not only do they not worry about it, they encourage the child's many mistakes as he learns to speak. Oh, and the good news is that I have yet to meet an adult who still calls his father "da-da."

Isn't it true that we learn best through our mistakes? Skinned knees are a part of learning to ride a bike. Burnt meals are a part of learning to cook. Think back to your first year of teaching. If you're a first-year teacher, think back to yesterday. Didn't you make mistakes? No matter how long you've been teaching, you will still make mistakes. So why is it that, in many classrooms, mistakes seem unacceptable? Why is it that we don't hear enough teachers saying, "Great! You made a mistake. Now let's see what we can learn from it." I am not suggesting that we never point out students' mistakes. I am suggesting that we make it *okay* to make mistakes in our classrooms. We should encourage students to take risks, make mistakes, and then learn from those mistakes. The greatest mistake any student can make is to stop trying for fear of failing. And the greatest mistake any teacher can make is to encourage that type of behavior.

✔ **Ask Yourself:** Do I ensure that my classroom is a haven for student risk-taking?

Tip 99
Refuse to Give Up on Any Student

> I promise never to give up on you, no matter what you say or do,
> For I am your teacher and teach you I will,
> Even if you give up, I'll believe in you still.

It is when we think we have exhausted all resources that we should resolve never to stop trying. It is when a child tries our patience to the very end that we must muster even more patience. It is when we think we can't that we should. It should be with utmost resolve that we refuse to give up on any student. It should be with resolute determination that we commit to making every child successful, no matter what it takes. And when a child is not experiencing success, we, as teachers, must change our approach – and keep changing that approach until we find one that works.

Imagine being a kid and knowing, beyond doubt, that there is one person who will not give up on you, no matter what you do or say or think or feel. Some kids just don't have that person in their lives.

Remember the following:

- Every student is someone special.
- Every student deserves a fair chance.
- Every student deserves a capable, caring, competent teacher.
- Every student deserves to be treated with dignity and respect.
- Every student is capable of success.
- Every student has strengths that need to be recognized and nurtured.
- Every student truly wants to succeed.
- Every student craves love and appreciation, which every teacher should provide.

Find, in every student, the goodness that often lies hidden behind life's layers of protection. Find it. It is your responsibility. It is your privilege. It is your calling. Work your magic!

> ✔ **Ask Yourself:** Do ALL of my students know that I, their teacher and biggest cheerleader, will not give up on them no matter what?

Tip 100
Remind Yourself (Periodically)
Why You Chose Teaching

Every individual would like to leave this world knowing he made a difference.
What better way to ensure that legacy than by choosing to be a teacher!

Okay, so we all entered the profession of teaching for the same reason: the money! (Ha!) Seriously, I believe that, as teachers, we all share a common calling and a common purpose. In my training sessions with teachers, I often begin by asking a few teachers to share why they entered the profession. It is always inspirational to hear the same thing, yet stated in unique ways by each teacher. The prevailing theme? "I wanted to make a difference, to touch lives." And it never fails: Following the training session, someone always comes to me and says, "Thanks for helping me to remember why I became a teacher. I had almost forgotten."

In the everyday mayhem of our lives, we often get "caught up" in the negatives. It can happen in our personal lives and in our professional lives. **In teaching, it is sometimes all too easy to lose sight of our main focus, our students.** I once had a meeting with a teacher who just needed to "vent." The conversation went like this: "I can't understand why we've adopted yet another new set of curriculum standards. The pendulum just keeps swinging back and forth. I'm up to my ears in paperwork, and I've just been asked to chair yet another committee. The whole educational system seems to be going down like a sinking ship. When are we going to get a break? Why don't they just leave us alone?" After listening to her express her frustrations, I said, "Tell me what made you choose this profession." The teacher went on to share a touching story about a teacher who had influenced her life in so many ways. She said, "Realizing what a difference she made with me, one student of many, I decided that that's what I wanted to do – make a difference in the lives of children, just as my teacher had done for me." I didn't have to say another word. The teacher smiled warmly and said, "Thanks for reminding me of that. I guess I was losing sight of the only thing that really matters in this profession: making a difference."

> ✔ **Ask Yourself:** Do I realize that teaching is stressful and at times overwhelming? When I feel like I'm at the end of my rope, do I remind myself that I AM A ROPE – a lifeline for the students I teach?

Tip 101
Keep Your Rose-colored Glasses On

Wear the Title "Teacher" Proudly

"Oh take off your rosy glasses," says a teacher as she passes,
For she sees my new excitement almost like it's her indictment
Of her dreadful misery, my-oh-my-oh-my-oh me!
But another teacher passes who still wears rose-colored glasses.
She has worn them 30 years, for she loves the little dears
That she teaches every day, yay-oh-yay-oh-yay-oh-yay!
So my excitement's not for naught; I can love all days I've taught
And I know the choice is mine; I can cheer or I can whine
And at the end of 30 years, I hope that you can hear me loudly
As I still recite my cheers and wear the title "Teacher" proudly!

If, at any stage in your career, you lose your rose-colored glasses, it is probably time to find a new career. On any faculty (remember Mrs. Warn Ya from Tip 53) there are teachers who have long ago lost their rose-colored glasses and have simply *forgotten* to quit or retire. They are quick to find the new teachers and share their lack of enthusiasm for teaching, students, and the profession. Don't participate. Know, from the beginning of your career, that teaching is not easy. You will never be paid what you deserve, you will always have new programs, new curriculums, new "whatevers" to learn, and you will never have a class where all students do all that is expected of them. But that's no reason to lose your fire and your memory of what got you here in the first place. So don't fall into the negative trap with those who no longer love what they do. Here's a simple trick for defusing those who have lost their love of teaching:

Let's say that a non-rose-colored-glasses-wearing teacher approaches you and begins to warn you about certain trouble-causing students. Simply say, "Thanks so much for telling me about them. Those are the kinds of students who need me the most, so I'll give them extra special attention. You must care a lot about them to have shared their stories with me. Again, thanks so much." And walk away with a smile on your face. It works every time!

And here's one more trick:

Let's say that one of these same teachers approaches you with some type of gossip about a student, a co-worker, etc. Simply say, "I'd love to talk to you, but I'm in a rush to get to the restroom before the bell rings." That, too, works like a charm because they simply find another target on which to unload their gossip.

Remember, don't participate in anything that requires that you remove your rose-colored glasses. You can remain a positive, caring, hard-working, influential, effective teacher all the days of your career.

> ✔ **Ask Yourself:** Don't I want my students to love my class? If so, remember that students LOVE the classes of teachers with rose-colored glasses!

A Teacher's Influence: Section Highlights

◆ Remember that you will influence every student you ever teach. Whether that influence is positive or negative is completely up to you.

◆ Embody some (or all) of the characteristics of your favorite teacher. Embody none of the characteristics of your least favorite teacher.

◆ Ask yourself, "How do I want my students to describe me when they remember my class years from now?" Then BE the person you want them to recall.

◆ Inspire your students, every day, by acting inspired yourself, by expressing your belief in them, and by helping them to build on small successes.

◆ Keep an "I Am Special" folder as a reminder that you are making a difference.

◆ Welcome student mistakes and make your classroom environment one where it is safe to take risks.

◆ Never give up on a student. Ever.

◆ Recall why you chose teaching. Remind yourself of it on difficult days.

◆ Avoid the "negative trap." Maintain your enthusiasm and your optimism. If you lose those, your students won't stand a chance.

◆ Be THAT teacher – the one every student remembers.

Conclusion

I hope that this book has served to provide you with answers, with questions, and with inspiration. Thank you for making a difference. Thank you for touching young lives. Thank you for changing this world, one student at a time. Thank you for daring to teach!

If You So Dare

If you so endeavor to seek and to find
How to light a spark in one child's mind
Then you have endeavored to change the world
Far beyond just that one boy or girl.
For once one spark is lit, you see
It ignites a fire that spreads easily
And so by touching just one child
You took one step that spanned a mile.
For you never know just how far-reaching
Will be your influence while you are teaching.
So teach each one with caution and care
And change the world, if you so dare!

As with all my books, I welcome your input, your suggestions, or any stories you may wish to share for my future writings. Please feel free to contact me:

AnnetteLBreaux@yahoo.com
Twitter @AnnetteBreaux

BONUS SEVEN

This Bonus Seven section is taken from *Seven Simple Secrets: What the BEST Teachers Know and Do!* by Annette Breaux and Todd Whitaker. We have included it here because we feel that mentors and new teachers can use these lists for conversation starters, for goal-setting, and to simply – and most importantly – improve teaching and learning. The lists share what highly effective teachers do on a daily basis. Enjoy!

Seven Things Parents LOVE About Effective Teachers

1. Parents love teachers who **treat each child as if he/she were the teacher's child**. They trust these teachers to treat their children fairly. These teachers actually tell the parents, "I'll treat each of your children as if they were my own."

2. Parents love teachers who **keep them abreast of what's going on in the classroom**. They love getting updates on what's happening in your classroom. They love hearing about wonderful learning that's taking place. They love being "included" and feeling "in the know."

3. Parents love teachers who **make efforts to ensure positive communication**. These teachers send notes home telling parents of their children's successes, make phone calls to let them know of good things going on with their children, and keep them informed as to the progress of their children. This way, when a serious or negative situation presents itself, the parents are more willing to deal with a teacher they believe actually cares about their child and enjoys teaching their child. With less effective teachers, a negative phone call or letter is often the first communication between the parent and the teacher. Thus parents feel the teacher only communicates when something is wrong!

4. Parents love teachers who LISTEN to them. This does not mean that the parent and teacher always agree. It simply means that the parent feels as though he/she can come to the teacher and have open and honest discussions, even in times of disagreement.

5. Parents love teachers who don't give up on students. These teachers do whatever it takes to help a child succeed – from taking extra time with the child, to suggesting to parents ways that they can help the child at home, to keeping parents abreast of all the efforts the teacher is making to ensure success for the child – academically, socially, and/or behaviorally. Parents see these teachers as team players, not threats or inhibitors to their child's well-being.

6. Parents love teachers who challenge students, while making learning attainable and fun. Students WANT to go to these teachers' classrooms, not because it's easy, but because they feel challenged, loved, safe, and successful.

7. Parents love teachers who do not overburden students with lengthy homework assignments. Learning is done in class. Homework is quick, meaningful, and doable – meant only to reinforce what has been learned in class. Many parents do not feel capable of teaching their children content they, themselves, don't understand. And, even if they do understand the content, they are wondering why their child isn't being helped to grasp the content in class. And even if the child does understand the concept of the homework, no parent is happy when their child has to spend hours at night completing homework assignments!

Seven Things Students LOVE About Effective Teachers

1. Students love **teachers who are nice** to them. Students, at all grade levels, respond much more favorably to teachers who are nice to them than they do to those who are not. The old "Do unto others" rule applies to us all. But remember that students are not adults, and they don't always treat others the way that they would like to be treated. That's why they need positive adult role models in their lives! Being nice does not mean that you let students have their way and do anything they want. It simply means you deal with them, in good times and in bad, in a nice, calm, professional manner.

2. Students love teachers who **make learning fun.** Don't we all? If learning is fun, it hardly feels like learning at all. Students should not feel worn out and frustrated when they leave our classrooms. They should feel invigorated, inspired, and successful. That's why the most effective teachers create ways to make learning fun and exciting. This way, the students can't wait to return tomorrow!

3. Students love teachers who **help them succeed.** The same concept applies to sports. Players love coaches who help them succeed. No one wants to feel unsuccessful, so students will often give up for fear of failing. This way, they feel "in control" of the failure. But in the classrooms of teachers who make learning something new appear doable and who guide students and who stop at nothing to help students understand when they struggle to understand, it's rare to see a student giving up. At the risk of overstating the obvious, success really does breed success!

4. Students love teachers who **challenge them.** Yes, students welcome a good challenge, as long as they feel they can walk away from the challenge having accomplished something, having experienced some degree of success. They don't want "easy" and they don't want "impossible." In between the two are activities that are challenging yet attainable. That's where learning takes place.

5. Students love teachers who are **clear with expectations** – both for behavior and learning. They want to know what they can do and what they can't – what we do expect and what we don't – what we will and won't allow. They don't like surprises. They like to know where we stand so that they can better know where they stand.

6. Students love teachers who **don't hold yesterday's transgressions against them.** Quite simply, they want us to wipe the slate clean every day.

7. Students love teachers who can relate to them and their lives – teachers who **get to know them as people.** Get to know your students – who they are and aren't, what they like and dislike, what they dream about becoming. Help them to realize their dreams. That's what teachers do!

Seven Things Administrators LOVE About Effective Teachers

1. Administrators love teachers who **arrive prepared for each lesson**. These teachers spend a lot of time planning lessons with careful thought and attention to detail, ensuring that each lesson is designed to maximize student engagement, interest, participation, and success.

2. Administrators love teachers who **handle their own discipline problems** whenever possible (which is most of the time). These teachers rarely send students to the office, but when they do, the office takes their referrals seriously!

3. Administrators love teachers who **make every decision based on what's best for students**. Though there are times when it is tempting to give students "busy work" or plan activities that give the teacher some "down time," these activities almost never maximize student engagement and/or student success. Effective teachers know this, and they make every decision based on how best to serve the students, not themselves.

4. Administrators love teachers **who come straight to them, the administrators, with problems or grievances** as opposed to griping to other teachers or, worse yet, the community. No teacher always agrees with everything that goes on in his/her school. But effective teachers air their grievances privately and professionally, never in a way that could harm anyone or degrade the reputation of the school, its staff, or its students.

5. Administrators love teachers who **continue to educate themselves** and keep up with current practices in education. These teachers never "finish" learning, growing, experimenting, discovering. It doesn't mean that these teachers embrace something merely for the sake of change. Rather, they are accepting of change and willing to try new ideas. They are open-minded yet realistic. They are willing to change and grow with the times.

6. Administrators love teachers who **are excellent classroom managers**. The fact that they are excellent classroom managers is the main reason these teachers have the fewest discipline problems. It's not that they get the "good kids" every year. Rather, it's the fact that they have established clearly stated rules and procedures and they are consistent with their

management plans. Students know what to expect from these types of teachers.

7. Administrators love teachers who **treat every child with respect and dignity**. No matter how tense or tough a situation may become, everyone is treated, in these teachers' classrooms, with respect and dignity. These teachers even know how to reprimand a student in a nice way, meaning they remain professional and calm, attacking the problem but never the person.

Seven Things Effective Teachers Do EVERY Day

1. Effective teachers **prepare, prepare, prepare**. Their lesson plans are detailed. They never wing it. You never hear an effective teacher claiming that he/she doesn't need lesson plans. And you never see an effective teacher using the same plans over and over, year after year.

2. Effective teachers **treat every student with respect and dignity**, every day. No matter how the student acts, effective teachers remain professional, realizing they are the adults in the classroom. No one is ever treated in a disrespectful or undignified manner by an effective teacher.

3. Effective teachers **smile** – a lot. They know that students are in need of positive role models. They greet their students every day – making their classrooms feel welcoming and inviting. They smile during conversations with students. And they smile often while teaching. They convince their students that there is no place they'd rather be than in the classroom, teaching, every single day.

4. Effective teachers **are good actors.** No one always feels happy. No one always feels professional. No one loves every moment of every teaching day. Effective teachers simply use their acting skills to appear as though they do! They don't allow their personal moods or problems to spill into their professional lives.

5. Effective teachers **remain calm and composed**, especially in tough situations. They draw on those acting skills just mentioned. They realize that when conflict meets calm, it is more effectively resolved. Therefore, the more out of control a student is, the more in control the teacher must be.

6. Effective teachers **have clear rules and procedures**, and they adhere to these every day. They are consistent. The students know what to expect, and the parents know what to expect – so there are rarely any surprises. When people know what it is you expect, they are much more likely to do what it is that you expect them to do. Period.

7. Effective teachers **teach from bell to bell**. There are no "lulls" in their classrooms – times when students find themselves with nothing to do. Idle time invites misbehavior. In the classrooms of effective teachers, it is difficult for students to even find time to misbehave. The teacher keeps the students so engaged that the class is over before they know it!

Seven Things Effective Teachers DON'T Do

1. Effective teachers **don't yell at or intentionally humiliate** students. Ineffective teachers are often heard raising their voices in a desperate attempt to regain the control they so often lose. They also tend to do things like calling on students who are not paying attention in an attempt to embarrass them. Such approaches never breed positive results, so effective teachers don't engage in this type of futile behavior.

2. Effective teachers **don't gossip.** Gossiping about others can only serve to harm others. It's never a good thing, it never helps anyone, and it should never take place in a school setting. Effective teachers are not overheard gossiping about students, parents, or anyone else.

3. Effective teachers **don't take student behavior personally.** They realize that they are the adults; they are the professionals. Students will say and do inappropriate things at times, and sometimes those things are directed at the most readily accessible adult – the teacher. But effective teachers know that the second they allow students to push their buttons, the students have taken over. So even when their buttons may get pushed (on the inside), they never allow students to know this. Their outward behavior is always that of someone in control. Not "controlling," but "in control."

4. Effective teachers **don't rely on others to handle problems that could be handled in class.** They handle every problem themselves, unless the problem is something that absolutely must be brought to an administrator's attention. If it CAN be handled in the classroom, it IS handled in the classroom!

5. Effective teachers **don't play the blame game**, blaming parents, society, the administration, or others for challenges in their classrooms. They know teaching is challenging, and they welcome those challenges as opportunities for growth – growth for them and growth for their students. Less effective teachers act as though their hands are tied and that until society changes, parents change, and their administrators change, they are helpless to make a difference in their classrooms.

6. Effective teachers **don't stop learning.** It is simply not possible to master the art of teaching and to finally learn everything there is to learn about teaching. No one has ever done it, and no one ever will. The day you're not learning something new about teaching is the day you should probably

exit the profession. Effective teachers realize this, and they never stop learning to teach.

7. Effective teachers **don't give up on any student.** No matter what a student does, says, or does not do, effective teachers have no "stopping point." They don't throw their hands up in the air and say, "I give up." They actually believe that every student is capable, and they treat each student that way. Students know that these teachers will stop at nothing to help them succeed and that giving up is simply not an option.

Seven Things Effective Teachers Love About Teaching

1. Effective teachers **love that teaching is challenging**. Successful people, in any profession, welcome challenge. Because we want students to learn to accept life's challenges and tackle these challenges with courage and drive and determination, we, as teachers, have to show them how. Worthwhile accomplishments are never easy; that's what makes them worthwhile! Teaching is not easy. But there is no profession more worthwhile! Effective teachers live by this belief.

2. Effective teachers **love that students have a variety of needs.** They celebrate the uniqueness of each student, as opposed to trying to make them all the same. They use their artistry to find ways to accommodate the differences in students, knowing no two students learn exactly the same way. If all students were the same and learned the same, teaching would be a breeze. Almost anyone could do it. If all patients had the same illness and could be treated the same, almost anyone could be a doctor!

3. Effective teachers **love knowing how influential they are**. They want to make a difference in every student's life, not some or most. They realize they are shaping the future, and they are up to that challenge. They realize that they live in the hearts and minds of every student they have ever taught. Their influence lives on long after the students leave their classrooms. They take their power of influence very seriously.

4. Effective teachers **love involving parents and the community** in the education of students. This does not mean that they get every parent or every community member to become active participants in educating their students. It does mean, however, that they are continually making efforts to utilize parent and community support as part of their students' learning process. They realize that if they encourage the support of 100 parents and succeed in getting support from one, that's one more than they had before!

5. Effective teachers **love when the light bulb goes on in a child's mind.** They live for these moments – moments that can encompass the slightest or greatest of accomplishments. Any little amount of success is a big deal to an effective teacher!

6. Effective teachers **love the fact that they teach children**, because they truly love children. Less effective teachers sometimes act as though their students sort of stand in their way of being good teachers. It may seem like common sense, but in order to be a great teacher, you have to really love children!

7. Effective teachers **love that learning to teach is ongoing**. They love learning new and different ways to help students learn and grow. They don't balk at every new program, technique, or trend in education. They welcome change and are open to trying new things, always!

Seven Things You Can Do to Be a More Effective Teacher Tomorrow

1. **Greet students** every day, every class period. Effective teachers stand at their doors with huge smiles on their faces (regardless of their personal moods) and welcome the students into their classrooms. The students feel as though these teachers are happy to see them every day. That one action heads off many potential discipline problems!

2. **Do things in small bites.** Take one of your lessons that you've already planned and add one activity that will make the lesson more engaging for the students. Don't change all of your day's plans or activities. Just take one and make it better. Add another tomorrow and another the next day. Soon, you'll automatically be planning better, more engaging lessons and activities on a daily basis.

3. **Ask for ideas** from others, and give one new idea a try. Effective teachers are always borrowing ideas from their coworkers. Don't be afraid to ask for new ideas because you fear appearing incompetent. On the contrary, you'll look more competent – as everyone knows that effective teachers are constantly asking others for ideas and sharing their own ideas with others.

4. **Revisit your management plan.** Make sure everyone knows what to expect from today forward. If, by some chance, you've not been clear and consistent with your management plan, that's okay. Start over today. Become clear on your expectations, share them with the class, and begin implementing your plan on a consistent basis.

5. **Tell your students why you love teaching**. Convince them that you are happy to be teaching them. Effective teachers often express, to their students, why they love teaching and why they chose this profession. If the students believe you love what you're doing, they'll be more likely to "buy" what you're "selling."

6. **Teach even more enthusiastically than you normally do.** If you want to be more effective instantly, appear more enthusiastic. Even if you're normally an enthusiastic person, act just a little more enthusiastic today. The teacher's attitude really does determine the overall climate of the classroom.